CONSTITUTION
IN
CRISIS

Compiled by

Joan B. Collins

and

Kenneth C. Hill

CONSTITUTION IN CRISIS

Printed in the United States of America

Published by:
Hearthstone Publishing, Ltd.
901 N.W. 6th St.
Oklahoma City, OK 73106
(405) 235-5396 ● (800) 652-1144 ● FAX (405) 236-4634

ISBN 1-879366-82-7

Foreword

Constitution in Crisis is a book with a purpose - to have the reader understand the nature of the threat of a Constitutional Convention and to act upon that understanding to defeat this Con-Con! The book is in two parts with the first part being an overview of the problem. This is taken from two broadcasts aired on the Southwest Radio Church program with Joan B. Collins and Kenneth C. Hill. The second part is a series of resources provided by Mrs. Collins and Southwest Radio Church to assist the reader in becoming better informed and involved.

I have attempted to edit the program transcripts into an easily read form and to place the resources within easy reach. I trust that the end product will meet the objective.

Special thanks are in order for Patricia Jones who has typed the manuscript and has, once again, done her usual fine job.

Reader, be informed and be about the business at hand to save our Constitution!

Kenneth C. Hill
May, 1994

Part I

Overview

The following is an edited transcript of two interviews about the proposed Constitutional Convention with Joan B. Collins and Kenneth C. Hill.

Hill—We're going to be talking about the Constitution in Crisis with an expert in this matter, Joan Collins. Mrs. Collins lives in the southern part of the United States. She is a businesswoman and a Christian advocate.

Joan, we have before us the question of the Constitution in Crisis. How did you get involved in the fight against the Constitutional Convention?

Collins—My husband, Bert, and I have been involved for many years in issues relating to application of Christian principals to our daily lives. We have been concerned about those things. Back in 1987 or 1986, we became aware of the movement for a Constitutional Convention and we began looking into that, what it meant, and what it could mean to Christians in America; we became increasingly concerned. We learned that the first state to call for a Constitutional Convention did so in 1975 and by 1988 when we got involved, 32 states had passed calls and only two more were needed before a mandatory convention took place. We had known nothing about it, nor did anyone else for the most part. Very few people were aware of this.

We then found out that the reason for the call for the convention was ostensibly to attain a Balanced Budget Amendment to the Constitution. This is a very appealing and good sounding reason for a convention. Upon further investigation we discovered the risks and the dangers of a Constitutional Convention itself, in terms of what that could mean to the document itself. We discovered that the Balanced Budget Amendment was in fact a ruse by which those who want a new constitution were to ride in on its coattails to a

Constitutional Convention at which time the whole document would be subject to radical dissection.

Hill—Former Chief Justice of the United States Supreme Court Warren E. Burger, not necessarily a friend of those who would be considered conservative, said, "I have also repeatedly given my opinion that there is no effective way to limit or muzzle the actions of a Constitutional Convention. The convention could make its own rules and set its own agenda. Congressmen might try to limit the Convention to one amendment or to one issue, but there is no way to assure that the Convention would obey it."

Collins—Exactly. And over the years, the pro Constitutional Convention (Con-Con) lobbyists and politicians have attempted to dismiss the concerns about what they call a runaway Convention, but certainly the former Chief Justice of the Supreme Court is an expert Constitutional scholar and scores of other ones agree with him.

What he bases that opinion on, I believe, is what occurred at the first and only Constitutional Convention which took place in 1787. When the gavel fell opening that Convention, the delegates proceeded to disregard Congress' preset agenda, a limited agenda that was given to them calling for modification only of the Articles of Confederation which were in force at that time. They threw out the Articles of Confederation, i.e. they threw out the existing government at that time, and they wrote a whole new Constitution. About 50 of the 55 delegates at that Constitutional Convention were practicing Christians, so, the Constitution they wrote was rooted squarely in the Word of God and the Ten Commandments. It maximized individual liberty while at the same time limiting governmental power.

But to ensure then that the new Constitution was adopted, the delegates simply ignored the existing ratification rules at the time and wrote new ones which they then used to get their new Constitution ratified. And to be sure, we have been mightily blessed by that Constitution. There is no question about it. Many of us believe that the Constitution was God's gift to a believing nation, but there are absolutely no Constitutional guarantees that the legal precedent established by the first Constitutional Convention will not be repeated by the second one with the result being a new Constitution.

That is why Warren Burger and many other scholars like him say what they do. They say you cannot limit it. A state cannot limit it. A state can pass all kinds of limiting languages they put in to restrict the agenda to a Balanced Budget Amendment only. Some of them have said that if they start to get into anything else, then we automatically secede from the Convention. They have written all these things into their calls for a Convention thinking that they can indeed control the agenda, but precedent is the basis for American jurisprudence. The precedent that exists allows for the creation of a whole new Constitution. That is the only way to get a new document under the present Constitution, the only way— scrap the existing one and substitute a new one via a Constitutional Convention. That is why it is being fought for so hard and so many dollars are being pumped into this effort.

Hill—When we talk about the Constitutional Convention we talk about Chief Justice Warren Burger and other people saying we won't be able to limit it. What is the problem with that? Are there not just a lot of well-meaning and good folks who would be the delegates to the Constitutional Convention who have wonderful ideas and ideals? Certainly there would be no subversive preset agenda.

Collins—There certainly is a preset agenda as can be demonstrated by the existing Constitutions that have been written that are simply sitting there waiting for just such a moment as a Constitutional Convention. There are at least four that I am familiar with and what I can tell you in a nutshell is that all of them together do accomplish one purpose. That one purpose is to eliminate the allegiance of this nation to God, family, and country. To do that, they eliminate, for instance, the inalienable, permanent rights from God. For our inalienable individual rights, they substitute government-granted privileges, which are, by nature, temporary. They can be removed whenever the state decides. It is like a drivers license, when they decide to take it away, they take it away. The same thing would apply to our right to worship. They disarm the people.

All these constitutions that are out there have a provision for confiscation of all kinds of weapons from the people. So that weapons will be held only in the hands of the military; that is, the government. They control and muzzle the practice of religion. And they mandate government education. They also mandate population control. These are some of the basic things they do.

Quite specifically I can tell you from one Constitution which is the "New States Constitution," which was written over a ten-year period and published in 1974 at the cost of twenty-five million dollars. It was funded by the Ford and Rockefeller Foundations as well as other foundations. The writing of this had some very specific Articles in it, one of which was Article 1, Section A8. That was relating to religion. And I quote, "The practice of religion shall be privileged. No religion shall be imposed by some on others and none shall have public support." Well what does the law mean about impose? Does it mean parents to children? Does that mean preachers to their congregations? Does that mean you and I when expressing the Gospel, fulfilling the Great Commission? It can mean all of those things.

Another one with respect to education, in the New States Constitution, Article 1, Section A11, reads, "education shall be provided at public expense for those who meet appropriate tests of eligibility." Now if you read that carefully you can see that the opposite of that statement, the opposite of "education shall be provided at public expense," is education at private expense. Since it is at public expense, private education is therefore abolished. With a stroke of a pen, Christian education, home schooling, and every other type of private education is eliminated.

The same thing applies to their removal of lethal weapons, as they call it. In the same article, Section D8, they say, "the bearing of arms, or the possession of lethal weapons shall be confined to the police, members of the armed forces and those licensed under law." Those people who would merge the United States and the people of America into a one world community, and New World Order, if you will, need a Constitution that is compatible with other world constitutions and principally with the United Nations Charter. It cannot be a God-based Constitution that emphasizes individual inalienable rights from God. Someone who believes that he has a right from God to bear arms and protect his family is not likely to willingly relinquish that right. Those rights must be changed to privileges.

All the battles that we fight out there on vital critical issues are extremely important. Those battles against pornography, against abortion, against homosexuality, all of the things that Christians are involved in, we do so because we have a legal right to do so under the Constitution. That freedom is guaranteed to us under the Constitution. If we do not have the document - my husband and I call it our ammunition dump - if we leave the ammunition dump unprotected, it is a target of those who would control us. The Constitution is the only obstacle between us and total government tyranny. Therefore, it is critical that everyone, not just Christians but non-believers as well, that anyone who wants to ensure his individual basic rights should be involved in protecting and preserving the document that gives him that freedom to do so.

Hill— Joan is not alone in her opposition to the proposed Constitutional Convention. There are many people in opposition. For example, Concerned Women for America have gone on record against the Constitutional Convention. Also opposed are the American Legion, the National Rifle Association, the Southern Baptist Convention, Eagle Forum, and the Veterans of Foreign Wars. A whole list is available of folks and organizations that are against a Constitutional Convention.

Joan, address the issue of the states that have called for a Constitutional Convention. These called for the new Constitutional Convention under the guise of calling for a Balanced Budget Amendment, didn't they?

Collins— Yes, they did. Many of the states, and most of the legislators, had no idea what they were doing. They were told that this whole issue was about controlling the fiscal irresponsibility of the federal government, to control the deficit. They are still being told those same deceptions. A state has not passed a call for a convention since 1983 because we are so close to a Constitutional Convention, and because so many people out in the grassroots have now become informed and aware and are now fighting it within their own state. But all the ones that preceded 1983, were achieved in many cases without any public hearings at all. It was just a rubber stamp of a conservative-sounding cause to control federal spending. They had no idea of the true motive behind these calls for a Constitutional Convention. They didn't look at the method that was being proposed to achieve this amendment which isn't even a surety anyway. If there was a Constitutional Convention it is highly unlikely that there would even be a balanced budget coming out of it, because the whole agenda would be a new constitution. They have been royally deceived.

Hill— I have noticed here in the information that you have supplied us that of the states that have passed Constitutional Convention petitions, there are three that have withdrawn those petitions. What effect does that really have on the call for a Constitutional Convention? Will those withdrawals be ignored, or will they simply be sustained? What will happen?

Collins—The recalls are entirely legal. And the fact of the matter is if others of the 29 remaining states withdrew their calls then it would be very difficult for anybody to ignore. The fact is that a couple dozen of those states have tried. Some like Maryland and Pennsylvania have tried, four, five, six, seven times in a row to withdraw their call for a Constitutional Convention and have been unsuccessful. These lobbying forces are very formidable and have defeated every effort in exactly the same scenario in every state that has tried to withdraw. There are 29 active calls on the books right now.

The problem is the power of the tax-exempt foundations and the political lobbying forces, those people in favor of conventions who were part of the Committee on the Constitutional System. This is comprised virtually of the elitist of Washington career politicians and their front group lobbyists including the National Taxpayers Union, its head James Dale Davison, and National Tax Limitation Committee who is Lewis Euhler. Those people are very powerful. They wield a great deal of influence. There is a lot of money behind their efforts. They have defeated everybody's efforts to withdraw and they are working feverishly at getting some of the remaining 18 states to pass calls for a convention.
New Jersey, for instance, had a very precarious battle last summer. They were within a "hair's breadth" of passing a

call for a Constitutional Convention. This would have precipitated a call by Michigan which also had one in its legislature.

Then the thought was, "well they'll try to ignore the three legislatures that have withdrawn because if they are so determined to get a Convention they'll just do it and then thwart any opposition in the courts." It seems amazing the lengths to which they will go to get access to the document. It is not so amazing when you understand why they have to do it. It is an Achilles heel to the New World Order. If we retain the legal mechanism to kick out all of those programs and policies of the New World Order that we don't like, if God should bring revival to this country, then people would have a legal apparatus to restore America to its Godly roots.

Without the document, they will simply be locked up in jail for illegally protesting, or what have you. There will be no legal leg for a protester to stand on. So it is extremely critical that we preserve the document in spite of the fact that it is being ignored by the administration and by the courts. It still represents a very substantial Achilles heel. If it did not, there would not be hundreds of millions of dollars being poured into getting rid of it.

Hill—James Madison said, "Having witnessed the difficulties and dangers experienced by the first Convention, I would tremble for the result of the second." Joan Collins is a Christian advocate concerned about what will happen to our country, to our nation, to our future, if the Constitution is tampered with and rewritten as those who are calling for a Constitutional Convention would have it happen. Joan, what has been the history of this attack on the Constitution? Give us insight as to how it started and how it got to where it is today.

Collins— The Constitution has really been targeted almost since the document was written. For instance, in the mid-1800's the American Fabian Society wrote in its journal to the effect that the Constitution was too highly individualistic to allow for the gradual implementation of socialism. The Constitution would have to go in order to provide the basis for socialism to be installed. That has been a prevailing view of socialists, non-believers since the document was ratified. In the late 1950's I think the effort probably began to get to the document to change it starting with the World Constitution and Parliamentary Association who at that point was calling for a world constitutional convention in order to adopt a world constitution. They have been working at this ever since, and they have incidentally become very prominent. One of the Constitutions that is slated for inclusion in the Constitutional Convention is theirs. And they have written that. They have said that the Constitutional Convention in the United States would provide a basis for introducing a world constitution.

In the 1960s, following up on the WCPA, the writing of the newspaper Constitution was begun. It incorporates much and many of the precepts that were in the World Constitution. There were a number of books that were published. For instance, one written by Zbigniew Brzezinski, who you will recall was an advisor to Jimmy Carter, wrote a book in 1970 called, "Between Two Ages." And he was then tapped to be head of the Trilateral Commission based on what he wrote. What he wrote was that the celebration of the 200th anniversary of the Declaration of Independence would be a good time to come together in a Constitutional Convention to reexamine, as he put it, "to reexamine the nation's institutional framework in light of needed remedies." Others became as specific, and more specific.

Henry Hazlitt, who is currently the economic advisor to the National Taxpayers Union, and is a renowned conservative dating back many years, wrote a book which he republished in 1974 called, "A New Constitution Now," and that book is very alarming because in the book he says things like, quote, "an amendment could be proposed that would strike out everything after "We the people," and that of course includes the Bill of Rights. What he is suggesting is that the Constitution should be scrapped from "We the people" on down and rewritten which is, for a document that has provided more human dignity and more freedom for more people than ever in recorded history , for someone to cavalierly suggest that the document should be erased from its beginning is really alarming, but he isn't the only one that feels that way. There are countless others who wield enormous influence.

In 1980 the Committee on the Constitutional System came together, the CCS, that is comprised of globalists, internationalists, career politicians, headquartered in Washington. They include people like former Attorney General Thornburgh, former Secretary of the Treasury Brady, people like sitting Senators Kassebaum of Kansas, Moynihan of New York, and Hollings of South Carolina. The CCS was founded by members of the Council on Foreign Relations including Lloyd Cutler who has been pulled into the Clinton White House to try to rectify some of the Whitewater stuff. And others like Robert McNamara, William Fulbright, Douglas Dillon - people of enormous wealth, enormous influence and these people have come together ostensibly to study the Constitution, but have made proposals that literally abolished our separation of powers protecting the people from the government, and much more. So, this attack on the Constitution cannot be dismissed as coming from some kind of a fringe element, or radicals. It is radical to be sure, but it is definitely not fringe. It is establishment orchestrated, and therefore deserves our very closest and very concerned attention.

Hill— Joan, these seeming tinkerings with the Constitution are really more than simple tinkerings. You have told us about the establishment folks, those where the rich get richer, the poor get poorer, and the middle class and those that are interested in good government seem to be left out. I think it is more than that. I think it is a possible trampling of our liberty and of our rights as free Christians.

Melvin Laird says this, and he was formerly a Secretary of Defense, "The concept that a Constitutional Convention would be harmless is not conservative, moderate, or liberal philosophy. The concept is profoundly radical, born either of naivete or of the opportunistic thought that the end justifies the means." It seems to me that there are problems here.

Joan, who is going to govern? Is it going to be "We the people" under an Almighty God, or is it going to be "We the people" under shambles taking care of ourselves? Who is going to be governing?

Collins— Well, that is an excellent question, Ken, and that is the root of the issue. It is a war between God's law and man's law, and that has existed since the beginning of time, of course. It might help to explain that there are two forms of government, basically two kinds of law in the world as defined by an Englishman back in the 1700's by the name of Samuel Rutherford. He said that one is Lex Rex and the other is Rex Lex.

What he meant by that was that Rex Lex , which is Latin for "the king is law," means that whoever is in power - either the king, the state, the president, the military or whomever - he or it makes the law and determines what is right and wrong. Now Lex Rex on the other hand means that there is a supreme law to whom even the king or the state submits, and that law determines right and wrong. The U.S. Constitution is a model of Lex Rex because it is based on God's law and the Ten Commandments. It guarantees the permanent inalienable rights given to us by God. So no state or president or congress or court can overrule the law or interfere with those inalienable rights. These Atilla the Huns are around in three-piece suits today, not animal skins, are interested in controlling the masses can not live with a constitution like that - that protects individual inalienable rights. They simply can't do it.

So that is the reason that this movement is on and why it is so formidable, because man's law will be substituted for God's, man's irrationality, his illogic, his greed and lust for power— all of those things that have ruled peoples of the world for thousands of years and made slaves out of them is the same kind of law that will be implemented in this country. This is very difficult for us to believe, you know, from our experience-base of freedom. We take all those things for granted.

What I pray for is that people will suddenly come to the realization that those freedoms are not always going to be there. I think it was Madison or Jefferson who said, "the price of freedom is eternal vigilance." We have become lacking in vigilance, because we have taken our rights for granted. We must stop that, we must become vigilant, we must realize that there are people out there who will take it from us who have tremendous power and it is only the voice of the grass roots, the people, who have everything to lose. If they lose their Constitution, they are the ones that are the real losers. It is only their voice that can alter the momentum of this enormous locomotive at this stage of the war.

Hill— Joan, one of the things that troubles me in looking over the proposed constitutions, they all seem to be socialistic in tone, as opposed to individualistic, if you will. They all seem also to be not only one-world in their outlook, but they seem to be bordering to opening the floodgates to all sorts of evil. For example, section five of the New States Constitution, "there shall be no discrimination because of race, creed, color, origin or sex".

Collins— That's the equal rights amendment and/or the gay rights amendment.

Hill—That's right! And it's right there. That's just one example. Another one that I thought was very interesting was section ten of that same proposed constitution: "Those who cannot contribute to the productivity shall be entitled to a share of the national product. But distribution shall be fair, and the total may not exceed the amount for this purpose held in the National Sharing Fund." Oh, I tell you, this just drips with socialism. It is a horrible thing to think that my children, and/or my grandchildren, would have to live under such a thing, or that myself and my family would have to live under that.

Collins—Well, sure, and the whole health care issue is simply a precursor to that constitutional requirement because it is rationing pure and simple so that the elderly go to their rationing board and they say I need a hip replacement, and they say forget it, we don't have the money. Or I need a heart operation, and they say, forget it, you're too old, and there is someone who will be younger who needs it more. You give the government the opportunity and the authority to ration health care and then they have the right to decide who gets it and who doesn't. They make those choices and then you have all of the abominations that the Bible discusses that comes from that kind of thing.

Hill—How many calls are active?

Collins—Twenty-nine active calls on the books. Thirty-four required. For those who are interested, the reason why those numbers exist is because the opportunity to change the Constitution exists in Article 5 of the Constitution which says that the Constitution can be changed by two methods, either by two-thirds of both houses of Congress sending an amendment to the states, and three-quarters of the states ratifying it, which is the way we have ratified every amendment since the Bill of Rights. The other way is to have two-thirds of the states, that is thirty-four states by our number of states, petitioning Congress for a Constitutional Convention. So, these are the two methods. The first one happens to have been used in every instance to add every amendment because it leaves the central document intact. The only thing that is examined, dissected, reviewed, and surgically changed is the amendment itself, and when it is ratified, if it is ratified, then all the surprises have been ferreted out and all the consequences of that amendment.

But a Constitutional Convention is not just the amendment that is at issue. The whole document is taken down from its pedestal, and it is put on the table, and people go to work on it. That means that the law-of-the-land, which has always been virtually inviolate in this country, which has given the world confidence in our form of government and has enabled it to withstand a monumental crisis up to this point, is now in limbo. Who can have confidence in a country that is examining and is changing its own basic structure of government? So, in this already unstable world, in a country where we have horrendous problems, we then engage in a process that destabilizes the whole system of government. It doesn't make any sense. It is totally illogical.

But what it does do is provide a fertile ground for someone to step in and say, "here is a new constitution and it has been developed by all the great brains of the world, and they've got the solutions to all your problems, so just accept it." What are the people going to do? They are in the middle of an economic crisis, everything has collapsed. An increasing problem that society faces is that people are turning even more to their government, hoping that government will solve those problems, and the government is just sitting there waiting for that opportunity.

Hill— Joan, let's talk about how we can respond. What kind of a call to action can we respond to? What can be done to prevent the Constitutional Convention from occurring?

Collins— The first thing that any one individual has to do is inform him or herself. He's got to find out, request the literature, the resource material from Southwest Radio Church, and review it. Then find out where your state is in this. Is your state one that has passed the call already, or is it one of the states where lobbyists are working feverishly to get a call passed? You need to find out.

Call your state legislator. This is not a federal issue. You don't call your federal senator and your federal congressman. This is a state legislative issue, so call your local state legislator. You need to find out what his position is on a Constitutional Convention, and I wouldn't recommend doing that until you know about it yourself, because chances are you are going to hear something like, "I'm for a Balanced Budget Amendment." You have to be able to say whatever the reason is stated for a Constitutional Convention is irrelevant. What I am asking about and what we need to examine here is a Constitutional Convention itself, and method.

You need to inform yourself. Southwest Radio Church, way back in 1988 I think, published an article in which the ministry explored and stated the issue and were opposed to it. Way back that far the ministry said that. Not many organizations have become informed enough to take a position against a Constitutional Convention, but some have. For instance, Concerned Women for America is now conducting education groups. I think they have some material if anyone is a member of that organization. The National Rifle Association is extraordinarily supportive.

The American Legion worked with us very extensively in Florida in 1988 when we launched a grassroots petition, education drive through the churches in Florida in an education outreach. It was the most miraculous event in which I have ever participated because I do feel the hand of God was shown there because the churches came out en masse to protect their freedom to worship, and they reached people within the church as well as in their communities, and those people responded by contacting their legislators and telling them they wanted Florida's call for a Constitutional Convention withdrawn.

That was done in spite of the most horrendous lobbying. Planeloads of lobbyists came in from Washington to stop it. Full page ads were taken out in the major dailies in the state of Florida attacking everyone and anyone who had any opinion about a Constitutional Convention, and in spite of everything, still Florida withdrew. That is what is going to have to happen in every state. Those states that have passed calls need to withdraw them. Those states that have not passed calls need to give their commitment to you, their promise to you that they will not under any circumstances vote for anything that calls for a Constitutional Convention. If we do that the power of the people will work. It's a trite phrase that is turned around a lot, but the fact of the matter is that we don't have the money and we don't have the political influence in terms of the Washington establishment in force, but we do have our votes, and we do have our voice and it is a question only of whether our Constitution, our Bill of Rights, the gift that God gave our founders for being believing Christians, whether that is worth fighting and standing up for. I believe it is.

Part II

Resources

The Constitutional Convention "Con" Game (part I)

Reprint from the "Sound Money Investor" September/October 1989

The Constitutional Convention "Con" Game
by Joan B. Collins

"Miracles do not cluster. What has happened once in 6000 years may never happen again. Hold on to your Constitution for if it should fall, there will be anarchy throughout the world." Daniel Webster

New Constitutions... Written and Waiting!

Ten years, a hundred-plus prominent professors and attorneys (including Warren Burger, former Chief Justice of the Supreme Court), and $25 million later, Ford, Rockefeller, and other tax-exempt foundations produced a brand new Constitution to REPLACE the American Constitution. Although our 200-year-old Constitution has the unique distinction of protecting more freedom for more people for longer than ever in recorded history, these tax-exempt foundations deemed it necessary to rewrite it. Why?!

Their creation, the "Newstate" Constitution, literally wipes out our permanent God-given freedoms to worship, to "keep and bear arms," to choose private education for our children rather than forced or mandated government education, etc. It goes so far as to abolish all state boundaries and even change the name of the United States to the "Newstates of America!" Our unalienable rights (stated in the Declaration of Independence and guaranteed by the Constitution) are revoked in this NEW Constitution. Authority over man's freedom is transferred from God to the State through temporary government-granted "privileges," easily revoked by any government in power.

As if this weren't incredible enough, another wealthy tax-exempt foundation, the Committee on the Constitutional System (CCS), has authored proposed "Amendments" which abolish our Constitutional Republic, our Separation of Powers, and our "checks and balances" (all of which PROTECT THE PEOPLE FROM THE GOVERNMENT); to eliminate the "Independent" voter by mandating a Party slate of candidates (all or nothing), limit the power of the people and increase the authority and control of the Federal government.

Sound far-fetched? Maybe, except that these foundations are comprised of some of the nation's most powerful, wealthy and influential Washington-based career politicians. For instance, members of the CCS include J. William Fulbright (former Arkansas Senator), Lloyd Cutler (former Legal Counsel to Jimmy Carter and author of the recent Congressional pay increase proposal), C. Douglas Dillon (former Secretary of the Treasury and among the nation's wealthiest citizens), Dick Thornburgh (Attorney General of the United States), Nicholas Brady (Secretary of the U.S. Treasury), Senator Nancy Kassebaum of Kansas, and on and on and on. The Committee on the Constitutional System's goals are summed up nicely by James MacGregor Burns, (CCS Board Member and Williams College Professor) in his 1984 book <u>The Power to Lead</u>: " The framers [of the Constitution] have simply been too shrewd for us... If we're to TURN THE FOUNDERS UPSIDE DOWN - to put together what they put asunder [Separation of Powers} - we must directly confront the constitutional structure they erected."

How to "Confront the Structure"

1) the first step to a new Constitution is to "con" Americans into believing their Constitution is obsolete and outdated, it's "anachronistic, inflexible and irresponsible...dangerously inefficient even in a time of peace and fatally inadequate for total war," states "A New Constitution Now" (repub. 1974) by Henry Hazlitt, Economic Advisor to the tax-exempt, Washington-based National Taxpayers Union (NTU). One of many ways to condition Americans into believing the Constitution should be junked is to hold "town meetings" across the country examining the "inefficiencies" of our governmental structure, and analyze new proposals to "streamline" and correct its "weaknesses." Interestingly enough, the tax-exempt Jefferson Foundation has been conducting "mock" Constitutional Conventions in communities across the nation for the past several years, and inviting the public to sit in as "delegates." Of course, the built-in assumption of these meetings is that the "weaknesses" and "inefficiencies" of government are caused by a faulty, defective SYSTEM - not by deficient and incompetent PEOPLE "serving" in government! Following the "conditioning" process, the next step toward a new Constitution is "confrontation."

2) Amendments (changes) to the U.S. Constitution can occur in either of two ways. All changes since the Bill of Rights

have been added by one method - the "Congressional Amendment" process. Congress passes and sends proposed Amendments, one at a time, to the states, where each is intricately examined, debated and analyzed. If three quarters of the states ratify the Amendment, it's added to the Constitution. The ONLY way, however, to scrap and/or rewrite the entire document is through the SECOND method for change, avoided for 200 years because of its risks - an open Constitutional Convention (which explains the format for the Jefferson Foundation meetings.)

Dangerous Historic and Legal Precedent

The only historic precedent for a Constitutional Convention occurred in 1787. The 55 attending delegates
a) IGNORED their pre-set limited agenda;
b) TRASHED the entire existing government;
c) WROTE a NEW CONSTITUTION; and most important,
d) (to assure adoption of their new constitution), they IGNORED EXISTING ratification requirements, wrote NEW ones, and used the new rules to BYPASS the state legislatures.

Unquestionably, America has been mightily blessed by the God-inspired result, but as James Madison ("father" of the Constitution) commented: "Having witnessed the difficulties and dangers experienced by the FIRST convention...I would tremble for the result of the SECOND."

A SECOND Constitutional Convention hasn't been held in 200 years because, by virtue of the only historic precedent, nothing can stop a SECOND Convention from doing everything the FIRST did. The enactment of legislation, the ruling of the courts, the pressure of the states, even an uprising of the people, CANNOT GUARANTEE the second Convention wouldn't do precisely as the first and do exactly as it pleased. Those individuals and organizations behind the pro-Convention movement understand this profound legal precedent very clearly. Sadly, and by design, the vast majority of Americans do not. The American people are being deliberately led into a fatal game of Russian Roulette with their freedom and Bill of Rights, and for what?!!

Balanced Budget Amendment "Ruse"

The stated goal of a Constitutional Convention is to gain control of the federal deficit by proposing a Balanced Budget Amendment to the Constitution. Exploiting the legitimate and deep concern of patriotic Americans everywhere about the mushrooming federal debt, the National Taxpayers Union (NTU), members of the Committee on the Constitutional system (CCS), and others, with the help of a "gagged" media, have over the past 15 years quietly lobbied state legislators to call for a Constitutional Convention, ostensibly to add a Balanced Budget Amendment to the Constitution. When 34 state legislatures call for a Convention, under the Article V provisions of the Constitution. a Convention SHALL be held. It's mandatory!

By January 1988, 32 of the required 34 states had petitioned Congress for a Convention, and America was teetering on the brink of a full-scale Constitutional crisis. Did you know we were so close to a Constitutional Convention, an event that could destabilize our nation in the eyes of the world? Did you read about it in the *Washington Post* or *The New York Times*, or see or hear reports on NBC, CBS, or ABC? The silence of our "free press" was deafening! Only a cross-section of groups and organizations, like the American Legion, the VFW, churches and denominations (including the Southern Baptist Convention), the AFL/CIO, the John Birch Society, informed Farm Bureaus, Eagle Forum and a few others, had discovered the truth about the risks of a

Convention, had taken positions opposing one, and had started to spread the word.

Grass-Roots Efforts to Save the Constitution

Finally, as a result of statewide education and petition drives started and growing in hundreds of churches and veterans' posts in Florida and Alabama in 1988, a massive grass-roots coalition of people - Conservatives, Liberals, Republicans, Democrats, Independents, etc. - joined together and demanded their state legislators protect the Constitution and their freedoms by withdrawing their state calls for a Constitutional Convention. Those two withdrawals, thanks to aroused public awareness of the risks, were overwhelmingly successful. But since then, the pro-Convention forces have, as James Dale Davidson, Executive Director of the National Taxpayers Union (NTU) put it, "taken the gloves off" to stop efforts to save the Constitution. Other attempts to withdraw calls in 1988 met defeat in Oklahoma, New Hampshire, Louisiana, Maryland, Georgia, and other states, thanks to Washington-based "big shots" and "big money". Virginia's battle to withdraw lost by a tie vote in early 1989, despite a strong coalition of grass-roots support throughout the state.

American is within a "hair's breadth" of calling its second Constitutional Convention in history. Hundreds of millions of dollars are being pumped into states like Michigan, New Jersey, Vermont, Montana, Massachusetts, West Virginia, California and others across the nation to railroad calls FOR a Convention through state legislatures and to STOP withdrawals of Convention calls in other states. Oregon, South Carolina, Mississippi and more are all trying to withdraw against enormous pressure and lobbying from wealthy special interests. The object is to get the required (34) state calls this year, forcing a Convention on the people before they're fully awakened to its risks.

The SAFE Solution to the Deficit

Anyone who truly believes this is about a balanced budget isn't facing reality. The solution to the budget deficit is very simple, as expressed in the November 1985 issue of the *Oakland [Michigan] Business Monthly*: "If this issue is so important that some would consider a Constitutional Convention - potentially endangering that document, no matter how remote that danger is - then perhaps it ought to become the sole issue of Congressional elections.... We figure it would be much better to dump out a few Congressional seats and rewrite the legislative roster to get the Balanced Budget Amendment, than to dump out a few Constitutional provisions or rewrite a few fundamental tenets of our nation."

The best solution is usually the simplest! So why hasn't this one been tried?! Why haven't the special interest groups spent their millions on making a public campaign issue out of the Balanced Budget Amendment? Why haven't they targeted the districts of those FEW members of Congress who voted against the Amendment when it last came before Congress? Surely, it wouldn't take much "prodding" by the voting public to convince a few more Congressional representatives to support the Amendment, so it could get through Congress! Once passed, it would go to the states for almost certain ratification. It's totally irresponsible to risk losing the Constitution and every American's freedom to get control of federal spending, when that objective can (and should) be accomplished the SAME, SAFE way all other changes to the Constitution have been attained - through the "Congressional Amendment" process.

It's Up to YOU to Save Your Constitution!

To SAVE The Constitution, YOU must fight a Convention, educate others, and convince your state legislators to VOTE AGAINST a Constitutional Convention. The Constitution belongs to the PEOPLE; if it's to be saved, it'll be saved by the PEOPLE (with God's help, who inspired its writing). An educational videotape, "The Constitution in Crisis," is available for $6.00 plus $2.00 postage. Order the tape, show it to your friends, family, neighbors, church, clubs, etc., and then maybe...through prayer, we may have a chance. There's very little time left, so without your involvement, there's virtually no hope. Write today for the video, sample petition and resource documentation to: Joan and Bert Collins, 5737 Corporate Way, West Palm Beach, FL 33407, (407) 689-8222.

The TARGET of a Constitutional Convention is the CONSTITUTION - NOT the DEFICIT!!!

Mrs. Collins, a Florida businesswoman and Christian Life advocate, has extensively researched the Constitutional Convention and is committed to exposing its profound threat to America's God-given freedom. This article was reprinted with permission from **The Counsel of Chalcedon**.

The Constitutional Convention "Con" Game (part II)

May 1993

WHO?? WHAT?? WHY?? WHEN??

Brief answers to these questions sum up "Con-Con's" meaning, purpose and agenda, while alerting loyal Americans to oppose the planned dissolution of our 200-year-old U.S. Constitution.

WHO??

Our present Constitution belongs to us...the PEOPLE. In NO WAY will a NEW Constitution, designed by the elite, be "Of The People!" Overlapping, interlocking, networking, powerful organizations of Washington "insiders," career politicians, elitists and state lobbying "front" groups have (for 18 years) pushed for a Constitutional Convention because it is the only way for them to obtain a new Constitution, benefiting their special interests and not the best interests of all Americans. Some influential Constitution "revisionists" include:

—Committee on the Constitutional System (CCS) (founded by key members of the **COUNCIL ON FOREIGN RELATIONS [CFR]** and **TRILATERAL COMMISSION [TLC]** and funded by Ford, Rockefeller, American Express and Hewlett Foundations). Directors include: Sens. N. Kassebaum* and Moynihan* (CFR), former Atty. Genl. R. Thornburgh* (CFR & National Taxpayers Unions), former Secys. of the Treasury N. Brady* (CFR) and D. Dillon* (CFR), former Secy. of Defense R. McNamara* (CFR/TLC), former Secy. of Transportation W. Coleman* (CFR/TLC), former Govs. L. Collins* of Florida and L. Holston* of Virginia, ex-Pres. Carter's Legal Counsel, L. Cutler* (CFR), Corporation for Public Broadcasting head Sharon Rockefeller, former Ambassador to the U.N., D. McHenry* (CFR), former Communications Workers Union head G. Watts (CFR/TLC).

—Career Politicians (elitist Republicans AND Democrats) — ex-Pres. Bush* (former CFR/TLC), Independent Party Candidate H.R. Perot (CFR), Sens. R. Dole*, O. Hatch*, D. DeConcini*, former Arkansas Sen. (and Pres. Clinton {CFR} "mentor") J.W. Fulbright* (CFR), former Budget Office Director W. Miller* (CFR), former Chairperson, Republican Natl. Committee, M. Smith.

—State Legislative Lobbyists— NTU, (National Taxpayers Union), James Dale Davidson, Chairman, R. Thornburgh (CFR), Cmte co-chairman; **NTLC** (National Tax Limitation Committee), Lewis Euhler, President, Prof. A. Wildavsky (CFR), Advisor; and **ALEC** (American Legislative Exchange Council), John Armor, Legislative Lobbyist.

—"One-Worlders" (most CFR members): Globalists, "New World Order" planners, Trilateralists, Order of Skull and Bones, Transnationalists, Bilderbergers, Geopoliticians, Club of Rome and Bohemian Club Members.

—Americans for a Constitutional Convention, Inc.— Barry Krusch, Dir., and author of The 21st Century Constitution (drops pretense of a Constitutional Convention "limited" to a single Amendment and openly calls for a Con-Con to shred and replace the entire existing Constitution with a new version.)

[*In spite of sworn oath(s) to uphold, defend and protect the Constitution, SO HELP (HIM/HER) GOD.]

WHAT???

—Article V of the U.S. Constitution: [a] "...Congress...shall propose amendments or" [b] "...shall call a Convention for proposing amendments...". ALL Constitutional amendments since the Bill of Rights were added by [a] above. WHY??

—1791—The only Constitutional Convention, [b] above, in history! Delegates at that Convention:

    a. **ignored** a preset "limited" agenda to revise the Articles of Confederation

    b. **threw out** the existing government (the Articles)

    c. **wrote a NEW Constitution** (the one we have had ever since)

    d. **wrote new ratifying rules**, assuring states' approval.

<u>**Precedence**</u> is fundamental to America's judicial system. Events legally sanctioned in the past can be legally repeated in the future. Looking, then, at precedents a-d above of the 1791 Convention, it's clear that a Con-Con cannot be limited to adding an Amendment; rather, it's the legal pathway to a whole new constitution. That's why a second Convention has never been called and why Constitutional experts like former **Chief Justice of the Supreme Court, Warren Burger**, affirms that "there is no way to muzzle" a Convention—once it opens, the delegates can <u>legally</u> repeat precedents. And, the first precedent, [a] above, calls for ignoring any attempt

to "limit" a Convention.

WHY???

1) **Publicly-Promoted Reasons for Con-Con** ("good-sounding" reasons for gaining public support): to add a Balanced Budget Amendment to the Constitution, to add a Term Limitation Amendment on holding public office, to revoke the right to keep and bear arms, to add a "Gay Rights" Amendment, to add a Pro-Abortion Amendment, to add the "Equal Rights" Amendment, to add a "Human Life" Amendment, etc.—each of which could be added like all previous Amendments without a Constitutional Convention.

2) **Published Objective of the CCS (Committee on the Constitutional System)**: To install a revised Constitution that will dissolve our Constitutional Republic and substitute a Parliamentary system of fewer elective (more appointed) offices, abolish "check and balances" between governmental branches, increase Presidential powers, lengthen Congressional terms of office, abolish "Independent" voting, establish mandatory straight Party tickets, etc.

3) **Globalist Objectives**: The "New World Order" requires elimination of national sovereignty and subordination of all the world's nations and peoples to a central, all-powerful ruling class of elitists (based on Marxist theory that only 10% of the world's population is capable of governing the remaining 90%). Our present Constitution champions individual inalienable rights, national sovereignty, independence, and limits government under the Law of Almighty God.* If MAN'S LAW is to rule the world in a globalist society, then man's supremacy must supersede the supremacy of God. The U.S. Constitution and the concept of inalienable rights granted by the Creator must go!

4) **Objectives of the NEW WORLD ORDER Constitution**: to implement a Constitution compatible with world community constitutions and the U.N. Charter, permitting U.N. taxation of U.S. citizens, controlling the practice of religion, abolishing private property rights, disarming the American people, abolishing Christian education, subjecting the people to a one-world police force. In short, a new constitution will abolish God-given inalienable rights and replace them with government-granted "privileges" (i.e. to worship, to assemble, to trial by jury, to dissent, to keep and bear arms). By definition, a "privilege" is temporary—revocable by the political authority in power—while God-given "inalienable" rights are permanent, no political authority having the power to revoke them. "Inalienable rights" (as in our Bill of Rights) are **not** included in any of the new Constitutions that are written and waiting for a Constitutional Convention.

(*John Quincy Adams said American government "...connected into one indissoluble bond the principles of civil government and the principles of Christianity.")

WHEN???
—*Article V, U.S. Constitution*: "...the Congress..on the application of the legislatures of 2/3 of the several states shall call a convention for proposing amendments..."

"Two thirds" is __34 states__. Thirty-two had passed state calls by 1984. None has passed a call since then, and (3) state legislatures in hard-fought battles officially withdrew their calls by 1990, leaving __29 "active" calls__.

32 States Have Called for a Constitutional Convention To Pass A Balanced Budget Amendment (34 Needed): Alabama, Alaska,

Arkansas, Arizona, Colorado, Delaware, Florida, Georgia, Idaho, Indiana, Iowa, Kansas, Louisiana, Maryland, Mississippi, Missouri, Nebraska, Nevada, New Hampshire, New Mexico, N. Carolina, N. Dakota, Oklahoma, Oregon, Pennsylvania, S. Carolina, S. Dakota, Tennessee, Texas, Utah, Virginia, Wyoming

3 States Withdrew Their Con-Con Calls: Florida, Alabama, Louisiana

18 States Have Not Yet Called: California, Connecticut, Hawaii, Illinois, Kentucky, Maine, Massachusetts, Michigan, Minnesota, Montana, New Jersey, New York, Ohio, Rhode Island, Vermont, Washington, West Virginia, Wisconsin.

As the stage is intentionally set by deteriorating economic/political/societal conditions, One-Worlders and New World Order elitists sense victory is close, and they're right! They say the nation's problems are due to a faulty SYSTEM—not faulty PEOPLE IN the system. They cry for CHANGE, meaning to radically alter a system that has guaranteed more freedom for more people for longer than ever in recorded history. Full-time lobbyists funded by major foundations and powerful Washington politicians using taxpayer funds are aggressively pursuing Con-Con calls in (18) states that haven't yet called and are blocking withdrawals by at least (20) others (Oklahoma, Kansas, S. Carolina, Oregon, Utah, Pennsylvania, Nevada, Maryland, etc.), all under the guise of a Balanced Budget Amendment. Strategically, the (3) state withdrawals are being ignored! Lobbyists are deceiving state legislators that (32) "active" calls still exist, instead of (29), and that only (2) more are required to call a Convention. If/when (2) more states pass calls, the plan is, simply, to announce a Convention, despite resulting legal challenges. However, if more states successfully withdraw calls, withdrawals will be much more difficult to ignore.

At no time in the lobbying process is the actual planned agenda for Con-Con revealed to state legislators. (Our "free" press should tell the truth about Con-Con, but don't look to the media for help. The networks, major dailies, and periodicals are owned and controlled by the very same elitist Council on Foreign Relations [CFR] members seeking world government, U.S. subordination to world authority, and a new Constitution.)

<u>THERE IS LITTLE TIME LEFT TO ACT</u>

If Americans do not awaken to this threat to their Constitution, they will awaken one day soon to the most profound Constitutional crisis in history. Without the present document, NO LEGAL BASIS WILL EXIST TO OBJECT, DISSENT, OR REFUSE TO FOLLOW laws of the New World Order. The American people may lack the elitists' money, but they do still retain the power of numbers—**people** numbers, if they only can know the truth in time! Write today to Joan or Bert Collins for an "Action" packet, including resource materials, a 30-minute VHS videotape entitled "The Constitution in Crisis," and a sample education/petition flyer for alerting your friends and neighbors. Please enclose $15.00 to help partially defray the packet's cost and postage. The American Constitution belongs to the PEOPLE. God willing, it's up to the PEOPLE to save it!

STATES THAT HAVE PASSED CONSTITUTIONAL CONVENTION PETITIONS FOR A BALANCED BUDGET AMENDMENT

<u>STATE</u> <u>RESOLUTION NO.</u>   <u>DATE OF PASSAGE</u>

STATE	RESOLUTION NO.	DATE OF PASSAGE	
~~Alabama~~	~~HJR 227~~	~~8/18/76~~	WITHDRAWN! 4-19-88
Alaska	HJR 17	6/21/81	
Arizona	SJR 1002	3/9/79	
Arkansas	HJR 1	2/1/79	
Colorado	SJM 1	3/20/78	
Delaware	HCR 36	6/11/75	
~~Florida~~	~~HM 2801~~	~~5/6/76~~	WITHDRAWN! 5-88
Georgia	HR 469-1267	1/16/76	
Idaho	HCR 7	2/13/79	
Indiana	SJR 8	4/4/79	
Iowa	SJR 1	2/22/79	
Kansas	SCR 1661	4/26/78	
~~Louisiana~~	~~SCR 4~~	~~5/21/79~~	WITHDRAWN
Maryland	SJR 4	4/3/75	
Mississippi	HCR 51	3/20/75	
Missouri	SCR 3	5/26/83	
Nebraska	LR 106	2/23/76	
Nevada	SJR 8	3/7/79	
New Hampshire	HCR 8	4/26/79	
New Mexico	SJR 1	2/16/76	
North Carolina	SJR 1	1/25/79	
North Dakota	SCR 4018	2/24/75	
Oklahoma	HJR 1049	4/6/76	

Oregon	SJM 2	6/16/77	
Pennsylvania	HR 236	11/9/76	
South Carolina	S 1024	5/16/78	
South Dakota	SJR 1		1/29/79
Tennessee	HJR 22		3/24/77
Texas	HCR 31		5/30/77
Utah	HJR 12		2/1/79
Virginia	HJR 168		3/3/77
Wyoming	EJR 1		2/14/77

ORGANIZATIONS OPPOSING A CONSTITUTIONAL CONVENTION

Partial List

CONCERNED WOMEN FOR AMERICA
AMERICAN LEGION
NATIONAL RIFLE ASSOCIATION
SOUTHERN BAPTIST CONVENTION
EAGLE FORUM
VETERANS OF FOREIGN WARS (VFW)
JOHN BIRCH SOCIETY
General Board, UNITED METHODIST Church
Virginia FARM BUREAU
National Conference of CATHOLIC CHARITIES
National Board, YWCA
LUTHERAN COUNCIL, U.S.A.
UNITED CHURCH OF CHRIST
GUN OWNERS OF AMERICA, Virginia Chapter
BAPTIST JOINT COMMITTEE on Public Affairs
DAUGHTERS (AND SONS) OF THE AMERICAN
REVOLUTION (DAR/SAR)
General Conference of SEVENTH-DAY ADVENTISTS
Virginia ASSEMBLY OF INDEPENDENT BAPTISTS

Proposed New Constitution for THE NEWSTATES OF AMERICA

<u>Excerpts</u> from new, replacement Constitution, costing $25 million in funding by Ford and other Tax-exempt Foundations.

What you are about to read is true. It can happen, unless we stop it. To be aware is to care, and to care is to act.

<u>In 1964, the writing of a new constitution for America began, at a tax-exempt foundation</u> with the misleading name, Center for the Study of Democratic Institutions.

The people who took it upon themselves to write this new constitution on our behalf were, of course, not elected representatives, or in any other way our representatives. As a tax-exempt foundation, they were able to do political work on what amounts to a subsidy taken from your taxes, but you and I were never asked if we wanted a new constitution written. Indeed, only a very tiny fraction of the people of the United States even know that it exists: it has been made known to practically no one except a select category of influential people whose views and interest generally coincide with those of the people who wrote it. The American people as a whole are still in the dark about it, and this situation is deliberate. It is therefore truly a "secret" constitution.

This model constitution took ten years to write, drawing upon the efforts of more than 100 people. A preliminary version was published in 1970 and given exposure in limited circles. But, in 1974, an essentially final version was quietly published in a book entitled, *"The Emerging Constitution,"* by Rexford G. Tugwell (Harper & Row, $20), the man who directed the formulation of the new constitution. It is the fortieth draft. During most of the time that their constitution was being written, the Center for the Study of Democratic Institutions was lavishly funded to the tune of $2,500,000 annually.

Judge the product for yourself, based not only on the reading of the document itself, but also on the review and commentary.

A PROPOSED CONSTITUTIONAL MODEL
FOR THE NEWSTATES OF AMERICA

PREAMBLE

So that we may join in common endeavors, welcome the future in good order, and create an adequate and self-repairing government - we, the people, do establish the Newstates of America, herein provided to be ours, and do ordain this Constitution whose supreme law it shall be until the time prescribed for it shall have run. *[Editor's note: NO MORE U.S.A. — try "Newstates of America" on for size!]*

ARTICLE I
Rights and Responsibilities
A. Rights

SECTION 1. Freedom of expression, of communication, or movement, of assembly, or of petition shall not be abridged except in declared emergency.
SECTION 2. Access to information possessed by

governmental agencies shall not be denied except in interest of national security; but communications among officials necessary to decision making shall be privileged.

SECTION 3. Public communicators may decline to reveal sources of information, but shall be responsible for hurtful disclosures.

SECTION 4. The privacy of individuals shall be respected; searches and seizures shall be made only on judicial warrant; persons shall be pursued or questioned only for the prevention of crime or the apprehension of suspected criminals, and only according to rules established under law.

SECTION 5. <u>There shall be no discrimination because of race, creed, color, origin, or **sex**</u>; The Court of Rights and Responsibilities may determine whether selection for various occupations has been discriminatory. *[Editor's note: ERA! "Sex" can be interpreted "sexual preference"— so-called "gay rights" part of <u>this</u> Constitution!]*

SECTION 6. All persons shall have equal protection of the laws, and in all electoral procedures the vote of every eligible citizen shall count equally with others.

SECTION 7. It shall be public policy to promote discussion of public issues and to encourage peaceful public gatherings for this purpose. Permission to hold such gatherings shall not be denied, nor shall they be interrupted, except in declared emergency or on a showing of imminent danger to public order and on judicial warrant.

SECTION 8. <u>The practice of religion shall be privileged; but no religion shall be imposed by some on others</u>, and none shall have public support. *[Editor's note: Abolishes permanent unalienable right to worship. Changed to temporary government-granted "PRIVILEGE!"]*

SECTION 9. Any citizen may purchase, sell, lease, hold, convey and inherit real and personal property, and shall benefit equally from all laws for security in such transactions.

SECTION 10. <u>Those who cannot contribute to productivity shall be entitled to a share of the national product; but distribution shall be fair and the total may not exceed</u> the amount for this purpose held in the National Sharing Fund. *[Editor's note: Here's one for the handicapped! Woe to anyone "exceeding" his "share!"]*

SECTION 11. <u>Education shall be provided at public expense for those who meet appropriate test of eligibility.</u> *[Editor's note: The END of all private (Christian) education. No choice for your child.]*

SECTION 12. No person shall be deprived of life, liberty, or property without due process of law. No property shall be taken without compensation.

SECTION 13. Legislatures shall define crimes and conditions requiring restraint, but confinement shall not be for punishment; and, when possible, there shall be preparation for return to freedom.

SECTION 14. No person shall be placed twice in jeopardy for the same offense.

SECTION 15. Writs of habeas corpus shall not be suspended except in declared emergency.

SECTION 16. Accused persons shall be informed of charges against them, shall have a speedy trial, shall have reasonable bail, shall be allowed to confront witnesses or to call others, and shall not be compelled to testify against themselves; at the time of arrest they shall be informed of their right to be silent and to have counsel, provided, if necessary, at public expense; and courts shall consider the contention that prosecution may be under an invalid or unjust statute.

B. Responsibilities

SECTION 1. Each freedom of the citizen shall prescribe a corresponding responsibility not to diminish that of others: of speech, communication, assembly, and petition, to grant the same freedom to others; of religion, to respect that of others; of privacy, not to invade that of others; of the holding and disposal of property, the obligation to extend the same privilege to others.

SECTION 2. Individuals and enterprises holding themselves

out to serve the public shall serve all equally and without intention to misrepresent, conforming to such standards as may improve health and welfare.

SECTION 3. Protection of the law shall be repaid by assistance in its enforcement; this shall include respect for the procedures of justice, apprehension of lawbreakers, and testimony at trial.

SECTION 4. Each citizen shall participate in the processes of democracy, assisting in the selection of officials and in the monitoring of their conduct in office.

SECTION 5. Each shall render such services to the nation as may be uniformly required by law, objection by reason of conscience being adjudicated as hereinafter provided; and none shall expect or may receive special privileges unless they be for a public purpose defined by law.

SECTION 6. Each shall pay whatever share of governmental costs is consistent with fairness to all.

SECTION 7. Each shall refuse awards or titles from other nations or their representatives except as they be authorized by law.

SECTION 8. There shall be a responsibility to avoid violence and to keep the peace; for this reason <u>the bearing of arms or the possession of lethal weapons shall be confined to the police, members of the armed forces, and those licensed under law.</u> *[Editor's note: 2nd Amendment freedom to "keep and bear arms" ABOLISHED. All guns confiscated, and America disarmed.]*

SECTION 9. Each shall assist in preserving the endowments of nature and enlarging the inheritance of future generations.

SECTION 10. Those granted the use of public lands, the air, or waters shall have a responsibility for using these resources so that, if irreplaceable, they are conserved and, if replaceable, they are put back as they were.

SECTION 11. Retired officers of the armed forces, of the senior civil service, and of the Senate shall regard their service as a permanent obligation and shall not engage in enterprise seeking profit from the government.

SECTION 12. The devising or controlling of devices for management or technology shall establish responsibility for resulting costs.

SECTION 13. All rights and responsibilities defined herein shall extend to such associations of citizens as may be authorized by law.

ARTICLE II
The Newstates

SECTION 1. <u>There shall be Newstates, each comprising no less than 5 percent of the whole population.</u> Existing states may continue and may have the status of Newstates if the Boundary Commission, hereinafter provided, shall so decide. The Commission shall be guided in its recommendations by the probability of accommodation to the conditions for effective government. States electing by referendum to continue if the Commission recommend otherwise shall nevertheless accept all Newstate obligations. *[Editor's note: All existing state boundaries ABOLISHED. "Newstates" established.]*

SECTION 2. The Newstates shall have constitutions formulated and adopted by processes hereinafter prescribed.

SECTION 3. They shall have Governors, legislature, and planning administrative and judicial systems.

SECTION 4. Their political procedures shall be organized and supervised by electoral Overseers; but their elections shall not be in years of presidential election.

SECTION 5. The electoral apparatus of the Newstates of America shall be available to them, and they may be allotted funds under rules agreed to by the national Overseer; but expenditures may not be made by or for any candidate except they be approved by the Overseer; and requirements of residence in a voting district shall be no longer than thirty days.

SECTION 6. They may charter subsidiary governments,

urban or rural, and may delegate to them powers appropriate to their responsibilities.

SECTION 7. They may lay, or may delegate the laying of, taxes; but these shall conform to the restraints stated hereinafter for the Newstates of America.

SECTION 8. They may not tax exports, may not tax with intent to prevent imports, and may not impose any tax forbidden by laws of the Newstates of America; but the objects appropriate for taxation shall be clearly designated.

SECTION 9. Taxes on land may be at higher rates than those on its improvements.

SECTION 10. They shall be responsible for the administration of public services not reserved to the government of the Newstates of America, such activities being concerted with those of corresponding national agencies, where these exist, under arrangements common to all.

PLOTTING
TO
REWRITE THE
U.S. CONSTITUTION

by Phyllis Schlafly

An unreported meeting of about 30 persons took place at the Mayflower Hotel in Washington, D.C., on December 5, 1986. What they decided on that day didn't find its way into the press until January 11, 1987, when the *New York Times* published a page-one story telling only some of what happened.

Those who gathered at the Mayflower were some serious-minded movers and shakers who are plotting to rewrite the United States Constitution. They openly assert that our Constitution impedes solutions to many of today's problems and needs to be changed. This is no ragtag bunch of nobodies. It includes some of the most influential and important persons in America. A feeling of quiet arrogance pervaded the discussions; clearly this little groups sees itself as persons with the vision and talents of James Madison, Alexander Hamilton, Benjamin Franklin, and the other Founding Fathers who met at the Constitutional Convention in Philadelphia 200 years ago this summer.

One speaker admitted that they are known as "the parliamentary government group." Indeed, that is the purpose which brings them together. The aim of this group is to change the structure of the U.S. government by eliminating the Separation of Powers and replacing it with a European parliamentary system.

The real name of this group is the Committee on the Constitutional System (CCS). The organization itself has a very low profile; indeed, its name I.D. among the American public must be close to zero. However, the members are important, influential and powerful men.

The chairman and driving force of the CCS is Lloyd N. Cutler, identified in the *New York Times* only as "a prominent Washington lawyer." To be a "prominent" lawyer in Washington, D.C., the city with more lawyers than any other, is to be exceedingly influential. Lloyd Cutler is better known as President Jimmy Carter's adviser regarding the unratified SALT II Treaty.

Other important CCS members include former Secretary of the Treasury C. Douglas Dillon, former World Bank president Robert S. McNamara, former chairman of the Senate Foreign Relations Committee and leading Senate internationalist for many years J. William Fulbright, Senators Daniel Patrick Moynihan of New York and Charles Mathias, Jr. of Maryland, former Congressman and leading internationalist in the House for many years Henry Reuss, former Governor Dick Thornburgh of Pennsylvania, and James MacGregor Burns, a professor and historian who is often quoted in the *New York Times.*

The CCS and its members have been toying around with radical ideas for rewriting the U.S. constitution for about ten years. Now, because of the press coverage that will spontaneously be given to the Bicentennial of the Constitution by newspapers and other media, **the CCS is grasping at the opportunity to use the Bicentennial as a vehicle to make Americans dissatisfied with our Constitution and willing to accept structural changes.**

In 1985, the Committee on the Constitutional System published its own 334-page book called *Reforming American Government*. It is a collection of 40 papers on the Constitution. They purport to discuss the Constitution from many different angles, but it is clear that the persistent message of this volume is dissatisfaction with our Constitution. The discussion of the Constitution in these papers is centered around such topics as "problem," "**crisis**," "reform," "defects," "decay," and "risk."

The raison d'etre of the CCS volume is neatly summarized in the lead quotation by Robert S. McNamara which is featured on the back cover: "It is tempting to believe that our constitutional system, having survived for almost 200 years, can handle the daunting challenges it now confronts. But common sense warns us that it may not be so. These 'papers' are reassuring evidence that the creativity and sagacity of the original framers are still alive in this country. I hope they will help to stimulate a vigorous national debate over the best ways to meet the challenges of self-government in these difficulty years."

When we analyze that statement, we can see that McNamara is saying that (1) common sense tells us that our Constitution is not adequate to today's challenges, and (2) the writers of the papers in the CCS book have as much creativity and sagacity as James Madison and George Washington. The book also makes it clear that this little group of self appointed elitists, who think they can do a better job than the Founding Fathers, are planning on using the Bicentennial as a platform to achieve their goals.

For those too young to remember who Robert S. McNamara is, it should be noted that he leapt into the national scene in 1960 as the head of Ford Motor Company in the era of the Edsel, one of the biggest business failures of all time. He was Secretary of Defense from 1961 to 1967 under Presidents John F. Kennedy and Lyndon Johnson — the years when we lost our eight-to-one military superiority to the Soviet Union. By the time McNamara left the Pentagon in 1967, the Soviets had achieved parity with us in strategic nuclear power. President Johnson then appointed McNamara president of the World Bank, where he spent years giving away American tax dollars and berating Americans for not giving away more of our earned wealth to Third World countries.

The Separation of Powers
The Committee on the Constitutional System is very specific in its complaints about our Constitution and in its plan of action for replacing it. The CCS approved a report at the Mayflower meeting which asserts that the Separation of Powers between the executive and legislative branches has produced chronic "confrontation, indecision and deadlock" and also diffused "accountability for results." The CCS bemoans the declines of political parties and the increase in ticket-splitting by voters.

The Founding Fathers established the Separation of Powers as the fundamental basis of our structure of government. Our Constitution separated the powers of government so that each branch can serve as a check on the other two, and so that no one branch can become powerful enough to gobble up the others. This principle is what has preserved our freedom.

The reasoning is clear — and it has worked for 200 years. While the people should grant enough power to government so it can function effectively, we the people really don't trust government. So we must separate government into competing branches, with each functioning as a restraint on the others.

James Madison, one of the principal architects of our Constitution, believed that this original institutional design created by the Constitution was the best way to achieve the twin goals of liberty and justice. By "contriving the interior structure of the government" in a particular way, Madison argued, "its several constituent parts may, by their mutual relations, be the means of keeping each other in their proper places."

All the power granted to the Federal Government by the Constitution was divided into three branches: the legislative, the executive, and the judicial, each with its prescribed list of enumerated powers. As James Madison bluntly put it, the "preservation of liberty requires that the three great departments of power should be separate and distinct." The functioning of our American Government does not — and should not — depend on the integrity of those who hold the power, but depends on the institutional restraints imposed on their exercise of power.

Our American Separation of Powers is entirely different from parliamentary systems, such as the British, where the executive and legislative branches are combined. James Madison argued that the accumulation of legislative, executive, and judicial powers in the same hands is "the very definition of tyranny."

The President may NOT dissolve Congress, as the British Prime Minister can dissolve Parliament and call a new election. The Founding Fathers emphatically opposed allowing the President to have this power over Congress.

Congress may NOT fire the President, as the British Parliament can fire the Prime Minister. The Founding Fathers' experience with England, where Parliament was all-powerful, had convinced them that, as Madison said, the legislature has a tendency to extend the "sphere of its activity" and to draw "all power into its impetuous vortex."

Members of Congress may NOT serve in executive branch offices, such as the Cabinet. That would violate the Separation of Powers principle.

The Separation of Powers principle mandates separate and distinct terms for each federal elective office: a four-year term for the President and Vice President, a six-year term for Senators, and a two-year term for members of the House of Representatives. The different terms of office and separate elections for the President, and for Senators and Representatives, were one of the ways that the Founding Fathers limited the power of Congress.

Each federal elective office must be voted on separately. The President may not run as a "ticket" or "slate" with a Senator or Representative because those offices are in a different branch of the government.

All tax bills must originate in the House of Representatives, the body where every member must run for reelection every two years. The Founding Fathers knew that oppressive taxes, imposed by an unrestrained British parliament, were the main cause of the American Revolution. The two-year term of all Congressmen is one of our greatest guarantees of freedom. James Madison persuasively argued that "frequency of elections is the cornerstone. . . of free government."

The CCS Proposals
Now look at the specific proposals made by the Committee on the Constitutional System, and note how these proposals

would destroy the Separation of Powers.

The CCS wants eight-year terms for Senators and four-year terms for House members, and wants to schedule all House elections in Presidential election years. This would eliminate the mid-term elections, along with the Congressmen's biennial worry that the voters might turn them out of office. This would have the effect of forcing the Representatives to run "with' the Presidential candidate instead of asserting independence from him. Some CCS members even favor requiring the voters to vote for President and Representatives together, as we now vote for President and Vice President as a team.

The political reality of giving four-year terms to House members would be that the American people would have to abandon all hope of ever cutting taxes. As the Founding Fathers so clearly saw, the two-year term for House members is our best guarantee against oppressive taxes.

The CCS wants to permit members of Congress to serve in the Cabinet and other positions in the executive branch in order to bring "closer collaboration" between the branches of government. This is unconstitutional today under our Separation of Powers principle. Even the *New York Times* admits that this would be a "pronounced" move toward parliamentary government.

Many CCS members want the President to be able to dissolve Congress and call new elections, and for the Congress to be able to get rid of a President with less difficulty than it took in Watergate. CCS members haven't yet reached a consensus on the most practical way to achieve this goal, which is clearly forbidden under our present Constitution.

Many CCS members want to call a "special convocation" to re-allocate the division of powers among federal, state and local governments. The goal is to take control over the cities away from state governments and give control to the Federal Government. Control over cities is one of the powers clearly reserved to the states by the original Constitution.

Checks and Balances

After the framers of our Constitution in 1787 designed the Separation of Powers, they created an ingenious and interlacing network of checks and balances which function among the three separate branches. These checks and balances were designed to make the system work while, at the same time, preserving our liberties. Congress makes all the laws, but (with minor exceptions) they do not take effect unless signed by the President. The President can veto any act of Congress, but the Congress can pass the law over his veto by a two-thirds majority in both Houses. The President is Commander in Chief of the Armed Services, but only Congress may declare war.

The President can sign treaties, but they do not have any validity unless ratified by two-thirds of the Senators. The Founding Fathers were very familiar with the way the British king had exclusive power to make treaties, and they did not want the American President to exercise that enormous power alone.

The Supreme Court has the power of judicial review. It may not legislate or execute laws or engage in policy-making — those powers belong to the other branches — but the Court can nullify a law by declaring it unconstitutional. All federal court judges, including Supreme Court Justices, enjoy life tenure; but Congress has the power to take away or limit the jurisdiction of lower federal courts and of the appellate jurisdiction of the Supreme Court.

The CCS doesn't like this system, especially the restraints put by the Constitution on the President's power to make treaties. The CCS report states that "the ability to enter into formal agreements with other nations is vital to effective national government in an increasingly interdependent world." This is typical rhetoric of the groups that want to persuade the United States to exchange its independence for "interdependence" in some variety of world government.

So, the CCS wants to eliminate the two-thirds requirement for treaty ratification, and instead the CCS wants to require approval by only a majority of both Houses of Congress. The CCS's president, Lloyd Cutler, is still smarting from the refusal of the Senate to ratify the SALT II Treaty.

The CCS report complains that "over 40 treaties submitted to the Senate for ratification since World War II have either been rejected or have never come to a vote." Among those never ratified are SALT II and several United Nations treaties. This complaint clarifies the goals and preferences of the CCS.

The CCS wants to limit drastically the amounts of money that can be spent on Congressional and Senatorial campaigns. The CCS says that its purpose in making this recommendation is to reduce the influence of "interest group contribution." Translated, that means to increase the influence of Establishment-type groups such as the CCS.

This recommendation puts the CCS in direct opposition to our First Amendment rights, as defined by the Supreme Court in federal election cases, to support and contribute to the candidates of our choice.

New Faces, Old Goals

There is nothing new about attempts by elitist, establishment, internationalist types to rewrite the United States Constitution. The Ford Foundation-financed Center for the Study of Democratic Institutions at Santa Barbara,

California, hired liberal academicians during the 1970s to produce some 40 successive drafts of a new constitution. The original project was headed by Rexford Guy Tugwell, one of the members of President Franklin D. Roosevelt's "brain trust" during the 1930s.

The Center's proposals had the same goal as the CCS recommendations, namely, to give us a parliamentary form of government that could be more easily manipulated by the liberal establishment power-brokers. But the Center's proposals were so radical, and their rhetoric was so alien to the ears of Americans, that these new constitutions were not taken seriously by the public or the politicians.

The internationalists then made a serious attempt to use the Bicentennial of the Declaration of Independence in 1976 as a vehicle to rewrite the U.S. Constitution. The World Affairs Council of Philadelphia published a "Declaration of INTERdependence" and somehow persuaded 104 Senators and Congressmen to sign it, including such famous names as Senators Alan Cranston, Hubert Humphrey, George McGovern, and Walter Mondale, and Congressmen John B. Anderson, Les Aspin, and John Brademas.

However, this ploy was greeted by a torrent of criticism from other Congressmen, and it was dropped.

In the 1980s, the Committee for the Constitutional System assumed the leadership of the plan to rewrite the Constitution. The CCS has been working on its project to trick us into a new constitution for about five years, and started publishing its plans to rewrite the Constitution in 1983.

Pandering to Political Parties

The 1987 version, however, has a significant new addition. The smart men in the CCS apparently have recognized that it will be very difficult to sell a rewrite of the Constitution to the American people, who have deep-seated reverence for our Constitution. And it is rather difficult to amend the Constitution in the traditional way. The normal amendment process, used for all 26 existing amendments, requires passage by two-thirds of each House of Congress and ratification by 38 State Legislatures.

So, the CCS has come up with an intermediate plan to facilitate acceptance of its goals. The CCS has figured out a way to line up important support, namely, the power structure of the Republican and Democratic parties. The game plan is to convince the hierarchy of both political parties that their own self-interest is tied to supporting the CCS plan to change the structure of our government.

The CCS report, therefore, weeps crocodile tears about the changes in voters' habits in the last quarter of the 20th century. The CCS report identifies these changes as "one-third of all voters were registered as independents, and even among voters registering with parties, ticket-splitting became the norm." Continuing, the CCS report sympathizes with the party bosses about "the weakening of parties" and the fact that members of Congress "owe their election less to party than to their own endeavors." The CCS report says: "Modern technology has enabled candidates to appeal to voters directly, through television, computer-assisted mailings and telephone campaigns, and by quick visits in jet airplanes, all of which have lessened their dependence on party organizations and leaders. The key to these technologies is money, but candidates found they could raise it directly for themselves better than through the party organization. At the same time, interest groups found they could exercise more power over legislative votes by contributing directly to selected candidates rather than to a party."

Many Americans believe that these are constructive

improvements in the political process, and that it's a better system than dependence on party control. In any event, it's clear that these changes have taken place naturally in our free and democratic society. But the CCS is pandering to the political party bosses, appearing to sympathize with them in their decline of power, and then offering the party hierarchy a procedural method to regain the power they have lost.

The goal of the Committee for the Constitutional System is a system whereby legislative and policy decisions are made by a handful of people at the top who are appointed, not elected. It's so much easier to control the country that way, as every dictator knows. So, the CCS is willing to increase the power of the hierarchy of both political parties as an intermediate step in order to facilitate acceptance of the long-range goals to change the structure of our government. Here is the bait the CCS is offering to political parties.

The CCS wants to require Presidential nominating conventions to give uncommitted voting delegate positions to all incumbent Senators and to all party nominees for the Senate and House. This would give Congress a big voice in choosing the Presidential nominee of each party. Naturally, the political parties would like this, but this is contrary to the letter and spirit of the Founding Fathers' design.

The CCS wants to require all broadcast advertising funds expended for Senate and House campaigns to come from taxpayer financing, one-half of which would be allocated at the discretion of the two political parties. This would abolish your right to contribute to the candidate of your choice, and force you to contribute (by your taxes) to candidates you do not want. This would load onto the taxpayers the cost of Senate and House campaigns which are now totally financed by voluntary contributions.

Even more mischievous is the plan to allow one-half of all

Senate and House campaign funds (which all come from the taxpayers) to be distributed by the Republican and Democratic National Committees. This is a plan to pay off the party bosses to get their support of the CCS goals by offering them big money with which they can control party nominations and Congressional legislation. It would be so easy; campaign funds would be granted or withheld depending on whether the Congressman or Senator "cooperated" with the party. The Republican and Democratic National Committees would be able to enforce discipline over Congressional votes by the way they distribute (or don't distribute) taxpayer funds to candidates prior to each election.

The CCS also wants Congressional party caucuses to be given additional powers through stronger rules in order to formulate party positions and impose party discipline. This bait is ingeniously designed to increase the powers of Senate Majority Leader Robert Byrd and House Speaker Jim Wright, and thereby line up their support.

Adopting the CCS "Package"
The committee on the Constitutional System has a 51-person board of directors, and it's difficult if not impossible to get unanimity on anything from 51 people. So, instead of stating with finality the recommended changes in the U.S. Constitution, the CCS report cleverly presents what it calls the "desirable package" which CCS leaders hope will result from a discussion of constitutional changes. Here is the "package" which sums up the CCS's first step in changing us from a Separation of Powers government to a European parliamentarian government, which can be more easily controlled by the establishment elite:
"1. Adopting four-year terms for House members and eight-year terms for Senators, with elections in presidential years.
2. Empowering the President (perhaps with the consent of a specified number of members of one or both houses) or the Congress (by a special or regular majority of both houses, or

perhaps even by an absolute majority of members of one house) to call for a prompt election to all federal offices for new, full terms.

3. Permitting the President to appoint members of Congress to the executive branch without requiring them to give up their seats.

4. Allowing Congress, by constitutional amendment, if necessary, to place reasonable limitations on the total that may be spent in a political campaign.

5. Holding a federal-state-local convocation every ten years to make recommendations for improving the federal system."

How does the Committee on the Constitutional System plan to get this "package" adopted? The report says that the CCS "favors" the traditional procedure by which 26 amendments have already been added to the U.S. Constitution, but the report does not say that the CCS opposes the other amendment procedure prescribed in Article V, which has never before been used.

The United States is now perilously on the brink of being plunged into this other Article V amendment route — the calling of a Constitutional Convention. Unfortunately, 32 State Legislatures have passed resolutions calling for a Constitutional Convention to consider a Balanced Budget Amendment. If two more states do likewise, Article V requires Congress to call such a Constitutional Convention.

At that point, the United States Constitution would be up for grabs and open to any and all changes. We can assume that the Committee on the Constitutional System will be ready and waiting with its "package". The CCS members are men of power and influence who customarily enjoy wide access to the liberal media when they want it, and a respectful silence when they prefer to operate without publicity.

The CCS members are single-minded in their goal of restructuring the American Government, and are clever craftsmen with words. The CCS report opens and closes with words which obliquely urge a new Constitutional Convention to rewrite the United States Constitution. The opening section of the report states that CCS "honors" the great work of our forebearers " by seeking to emulate it." In other words, the CCS does not intend to celebrate the Bicentennial by honoring the Constitution which the Founding Fathers wrote; instead, the CCS wants to celebrate the Bicentennial by imitating (emulating) what the Founding Fathers did, namely, write a new constitution.

The CCS report concludes with the same theme: "The best way to honor the framers of the Constitution during this Bicentennial era is to follow their example." It is clear from the context that the CCS intends to follow the example of the Founding Fathers and write a new constitution; the CCS does NOT intend to follow the Constitution that the Founding Fathers wrote.

In this year of the Bicentennial, we should all follow the advice of George Washington to his troops: "Put none but Americans on guard tonight." If there ever was a time when Americans need to be on guard to protect our Constitution, that time is NOW!

Contact: Charles Kuszmaul
3230 Suffolk Lane
Fallston, MD 21047

The following was sent from an Ad Hoc Committee Education Outreach: "Risks of a Constitutional Convention"

Dr. Jay Grimstead
Mr. Ed McAteer
Dr. Paul Kienel
Pastor Paul Lindstrom
Dr. Richard Bliss
Dr. Ted Baehr
Dr. D. James Kennedy
Mr. Larry Pratt
Mr. Gerry Nordskog
Mr. Tim Wildmon
Dr. Joe Morecraft, III
Ms. Catherine Millard
Rev. Marshall Foster
Ed Payne, M.D.
Mr. Paul Jahle
Mr. Jack Caulfield
Rev. Christopher Hoops
Mr. Dennis Peacock
Dr. Bob Simonds
Nita and Bill Scoggan
Mr. Steve Carr
Dr. Larry Walker

November 1992

Dear Pastor:

WHICH KIND OF FREEDOM DO YOU WANT FOR THE FUTURE OF THE CHURCH?

U.S. CONSTITUTION
" Congress shall make no law respecting an establishment of religion, or prohibiting the free exercise thereof. . . ."
Amendment I

NEWSTATES CONSTITUTION

"The practice of religion shall be privileged; but no religion shall be imposed by some on others, and none shall have public support." Article I, Section A8

.

What GUARANTEES America's religious liberty? Freedom to worship was so precious to our Founders that they guaranteed its protection by writing the First Amendment to the Constitution. Imagine the Church today without that legal protection from government control. Suppose the First Amendment were replaced by the above-*right* provision (from a new, proposed, replacement Constitution, costing $25 million of powerful tax-exempt Foundation funding). This "Newstates" provision replaces our God-given (permanent) inalienable right to worship with a (temporary) government-granted *"privilege"* (much like a driver's license), to be revoked at will by the State. And, what is meant by *"no religion shall be imposed by some on others"* . . . the end of preaching and evangelizing?

But, why worry? Our 200-year-old, Bible-based Constitution is safe, isn't it? A total Constitutional rewrite is IMPOSSIBLE, isn't it? NO, it's NOT impossible! Today, America stands on the brink of a **CONSTITUTIONAL CONVENTION**, an event described by former Secretary of Defense, Melvin Laird, as "fraught with danger and recklessness," and an event which (thanks to media silence) few Christians know anything about. We are called to be vigilant.

Enclosed is a **News Release** from Ed McAteer, Founder of Religious Roundtable in Memphis, Tennessee. Also enclosed is an article entitled **"The Constitutional Convention 'Con' Game"**, explaining the profound risks to the Constitution of a national **CONSTITUTIONAL CONVENTION**. Critical points include:

1. A Convention is the ONLY legal pathway to massive/total revision of the U.S. Constitution,

2. Millions have been spent by huge tax-exempt foundations and political special interest groups writing NEW atheistic/humanistic Constitutions for America, while maneuvering the nation precariously close to a Constitutional Convention,

3. The Convention idea is "sold" with a good-sounding motive, i.e. to write a Balanced Budget Amendment to the Constitution. Yet, recently, the Nevada House, *unanimously*, exposed and repudiated that stated motive as a **deceptive** strategy to quietly bring about a Convention in order to **REWRITE THE CONSTITUTION.**

We are writing today with the fervent prayer that you will join our Christian coalition to "sound the trumpet" on the dangers of a Constitutional Convention. As always, in spiritual warfare, the time is short; the enemy, formidable; the resources, scarce; and the warriors, few! For a "Seed Sowing Kit" (including the video, "The Constitution in Crisis") to educate and alert your Church and community to protect their Constitution, fill in, tear off, and return the bottom portion of this letter with your check for $15.00 to the address indicated. There is NO TIME TO LOSE. Send for your education packet today. For, IF THE CHURCH WON'T STAND *NOW FOR RELIGIOUS LIBERTY*, THEN *WHEN WILL IT* . . . WHEN IT'S TOO LATE?!! May God bless our efforts to his Glory.

Contact: Joan B. Collins, National Coordinator
Ad Hoc Committee Education Outreach
5737 Corporate Way, West Palm Beach FL 33407
(Tel.) 407-689-8222

NEWS RELEASE

THIS IS A "RED ALERT"
FOR IMMEDIATE RELEASE
ISSUED: July - August, 1989
FROM: Ed McAteer,
Religious Round Table,
P.O. Box 11467,
Memphis TN 38111
901-458-3795

CONSTITUTIONAL CONVENTION PLOT
IS TROJAN HORSE
TO RELIGIOUS FREEDOM

Christian "watchmen on the wall" have unearthed an insidious hidden agenda behind the unpublicized fifteen-year-old drive for a Federal Constitutional Convention, according to Ed McAteer, founder of the Religious Round Table, headquartered in Memphis, Tennessee. Ed McAteer stated today that he has been informed that an abundance of evidence has been discovered and assembled which convincingly supports the conclusion that the real power structure and elitist political groups pushing for a Constitutional Convention are after far more than a so-called Balanced Budget Amendment.

Since as early as 1964, Ed McAteer explains, committees have been created to dissect the United States Constitution. Radical change Amendments, in addition to a totally new replacement Constitution, have been written and proposed by several organizations. The new Constitution replaces the concept of inalienable rights granted by the Creator with privileges granted by the state. It includes a provision that "all education shall be at public expense"... thus abolishing education at <u>private</u> expense. Another provision mandates that "no one shall impose his religious beliefs on another"... leaving up to the courts to decide what is meant by "no one" and what is meant by "another". What do you imagine the courts will say about parents imposing their religious beliefs on their children or about evangelists and pastors imposing their religious beliefs on their congregations?, Ed McAteer asks. In addition, structural change Amendments, equally devastating, abolishing our entire form of government and substituting a parliamentary system, have been recommended by other groups. As laudable as the control of government spending is, we must not be deceived into the loss of our fundamental freedoms, Ed warns.

It is now reported that the goal of merely adding a Balanced Budget Amendment to our Constitution is the <u>good sounding cover</u> which is greasing the skids under deceived state legislators and citizens around the country to slide their support behind the drive for a Constitutional Convention. You see, a Balanced Budget Amendment by itself could be achieved through the Congressional Amendment procedure (the <u>alternative</u> method of amending our Constitution and used for all other amendments ever enacted), but a Constitutional Convention is the only way that multiple drastic changes, such as a new Constitution, can be obtained. The one-world advocates and the enemies of religious freedom, private Christian education, pro-life, and our Creator-granted inalienable rights know this, and so are spending millions of dollars and man hours to get a Constitutional Convention, Ed McAteer explains. Those who have researched this issue and uncovered the hidden agenda correctly point out that if this same money and man hours had been directed toward the Congressional passage of a Balanced Budget Amendment through the Congressional Amendment procedure, we would have had such an amendment by now. After all, the last time Congress was lobbied for a Balanced Budget Amendment, it lost by only (23) votes in the House and only (1) vote in the Senate. This alone should lead a prudent individual to suspect that the insatiable fervor for a Constitutional Convention is being fired by something far beyond a Balanced Budget Amendment.

I ask everyone concerned with religious freedom to avail themselves of the opportunity to examine this latest Trojan Horse in the battle against the Church and a free America. Reading the article enclosed with this alert is a first step. Afterward, I urge you to use whatever means you have of informing others. Be assured, this is not a partisan political or liberal vs. conservative issue. When you understand the roots of the conflict, you will readily agree. We dare not fall back from this challenge. If the United States Constitution is lost, little else of America as it was founded will be saved. I invite you to join me and religious leaders around the country at this midnight hour of battle. So powerful is the enemy, and so late the hour that even if we heed the trumpet call it may be too late. All who want to help should write or call me as soon as possible for reference materials, names of researchers on this issue, and names of others who even now are mobilizing as I send this alert to you, concluded Ed McAteer of Religious Round Table.

(The following is a format to follow to defeat the Constitutional Convention)

A PETITION

WE THE PEOPLE of _____(state name), are **FREE** because the United States Constitution **GUARANTEES** a **BILL OF RIGHTS** to every American. Today, 'We the People' stand on the brink of overthrowing our Bill of Rights and the entire U.S. Constitution by convening a perilous *CONSTITUTIONAL CONVENTION (CON-CON)* — the **ONLY LEGAL PATHWAY TO A NEW CONSTITUTION.**

RADICAL NEW CONSTITUTIONS await a CONstitutional CONvention — by law, now only (5) state calls away!! [Dateline: June 1989] 'FRAUD'!! Nevada's House overturns its 1979 call for CON-CON charging *fraudulent 'good-sounding' promises* led to their support. Since 1974 (31) additional state legislatures, also deceived by *false* claims that CON-CON will be *'limited'* to a Balanced Budget Amendment passed CON-CON calls. Americans now know the TARGET IS NOT THE DEFICIT; IT'S THE CONSTITUTION! Unwilling to play 'Constitutional Roulette' for ANY 'good-sounding' reason, FLORIDA, ALABAMA, and LOUISIANA legislators exposed the CON-CON sham by withdrawing their state calls.

WE ASK:
    Senator

_____

Address_____

_____

Telephone Numbers_____

_____

BEWARE THE CON-CON FRAUD!! VOTE TO WITHDRAW ALL STATE CALLS PASSED BY THE LEGISLATURE FOR A NATIONAL CONSTITUTIONAL CONVENTION (CON-CON).

PROTECT MY FREEDOM OF SPEECH, FREEDOM TO WORSHIP, AND FREEDOM OF THE PRESS.

"IF IT AIN'T BROKE, DON'T FIX IT!!!"

Please sign and return immediately!

_____(_____)
SIGNATURE   PRINT NAME HERE

_____
ADDRESS

_____
CITY, STATE, ZIP CODE
PHONE

IMPORTANT INSTRUCTION: (1) Sign and mail petition to address on reverse side (it's vital they're presented to legislators); (2) Call/write your state legislator and ask for his PROMISE to help; (3) Tell others and distribute petitions, so they can join in protecting their freedom.

FACT: AMERICAN LEGION calls (CON-CON) "a dire threat"; MELVIN LAIRD (former Secy of Defense) says — (CON-CON) "is not Conservative, Moderate or Liberal. . . (it) is profoundly RADICAL; *"USA Today* says — "The Constitution was written to protect 'We the People." Now, 'We The People" must protect the Constitution;" AFL/CIO says — "It could be the Constitution that gets scrapped!" WARREN BURGER (ex-Chief Justice Supreme Court) says — "There's no way to muzzle a Convention. Once it meets, it will do anything the majority wants."

FACT: Liberal/Conservative 'Convention-pushers" led by the National Tax Limitation Committee (NTLC) and NTU — National Taxpayers Union. NTU Economic Advisor calls the Constitution '...irresponsible...and fatally inadequate...' Massive Constitutional surgery is also proposed by the Committee on the Constitutional System (CCS). Members include elitist Republican/Democratic leaders (Attorney General Thornburgh, Treasury Secretary Brady, Sens. Kassebaum and Moynihan, and Council on Foreign Relations (CFR) members J.W. Fulbright, Robert McNamara, Lloyd Cutler, Douglas Dillon, etc.

FACT: Radical NEW Constitutions, funded by rich Ford, Rockefeller and other tax-exempt Foundations, are written and waiting for CON-CON. They revoke religious liberty, scrap the Second Amendment, abolish private education, eliminate 'Independent' voters (by mandating 'Party' ballots), abolish 'Separation of Powers' (which protect people FROM government), and bottom-line, substitute government control for individual liberty.

FACT: Constitutional change occurs by (a) 'Congressional

Amendment' (used to add ALL Amendments since the Bill of Rights), and (b) 'CONstitutional CONvention' (never used since 1787). To convene CON-CON, (34) states must 'call' for one; (32) have called! Because of its dangers, NO state has called since 1983 and (3) states withdrew. Nevada's House expunged its call FOR FRAUD. Twenty-plus states tried and failed to withdraw, thanks to arm-twisting power-politics from Washington 'big shots' and to a public, largely uninformed by the media.

FACT: First CON-CON was 1787. Its 'limited, pre-set' agenda was ignored. It threw out the existing government, wrote a NEW Constitution, and ignored existing ratification rules. James Madison ('father' of the Constitution) said because of 'dangers experienced by the FIRST Convention, I would tremble for the result of the SECOND.' This critical legal precedent means THERE'S NO GUARANTEE stopping a SECOND CON-CON from repeating what the FIRST did. That's why 1787 was the FIRST, AND LAST, CON-CON.

FACT: WE DON'T NEED CON-CON to get a Balanced Budget Amendment! Congress almost passed it! Simply changing a FEW Congressional votes will insure passage without CON-CON. 'Convention-pushers' tell us 'good-sounding' reasons to call CON-CON, but fail to mention its profound RISKS. *USA Today* says 'We The People' must protect the Constitution. YOU can protect it by STOPPING CON-CON!

For Info and Petitions, Contact:

_____

_____Phone_____

HINTS TO USE "STOP CON-CON" EDUCATION/ PETITION FLYER

With this flyer, you can EDUCATE family, friends, neighbors and co-workers to the TRUTH about a Constitutional Convention. No one can "sit this one out!" Saving the Constitution is EVERYBODY'S business!!

EDUCATION IS THE KEY, and this flyer will educate! Your state legislators will not resist powerful pro-Con-Con lobbyists without widespread support and action from constituents.

For info and guidance on launching a successful education/ petition drive, contact:

Joan B. Collins
5737 Corporate Way
West Palm Beach FL 33407
Tel. 407-689-8222 (weekdays)

CONSTITUTIONAL CONVENTION UPDATE

Pastor David Ingraham Interviews Dr. John Eidsmoe
from
Southwest Radio Church
P.O. Box 1144, Oklahoma City, OK 73101
(405) 235-5396; (800) 652-1144; FAX (405) 236-4634

David Ingraham — We're interested in learning more concerning the movement toward a constitutional convention for the United States of America.

John Eidsmoe — This movement has its basis in the Constitution itself. Article V of the Constitution specifies the means by which the Constitution can be amended and sets forth two possible procedures.

The first procedure involves sending an amendment through Congress and has been used twenty-six times. Once an amendment passes both houses of Congress, it is then submitted to the states for ratification. When three-fourths of the states ratify it, that amendment becomes a part of the Constitution.

The second method has never been used, though we have come close several times. If the legislatures of two-thirds of the states call for a constitutional convention, Article V empowers Congress to call this convention. The convention will then consider amendments presented by the states. Whatever amendments are passed by the convention are to be submitted to the states for ratification. This can be either by state conventions or by the state legislatures at the discretion of Congress. If approved by three-fourths of the states, those amendments become part of the Constitution.

As I said, we have never used this latter method. This method was proposed near the closing days of the Constitutional Convention in 1792. Several of the Founding Fathers were concerned that Congress would become a runaway institution, losing touch with the will of the people. For this reason they adopted it. This certainly has happened in the past, and I personally believe Congress is presently running out of control. When the delegates drafted and inserted that last piece of the Constitution, they did so rather hurriedly. When you read through Madison's notes of the convention, you find there was little discussion concerning it. As a result, this article is stated in very general terms, leaving many unanswered questions.

Over the years there have been a number of drives to call a constitutional convention, and for various reasons. None have been successful yet, but one did come very close. Following the reapportionment decision of the Supreme Court back in the 1960s when the U.S. Supreme Curt ruled that both houses of the state's legislature must be apportioned based on population, rather than by area, many thought the Supreme Court was dictating to the states what should actually be left up to the individual states. In other words, they should be able to decide how to apportion the houses of their own legislatures, and I thoroughly agree. This resulted in an attempt to put an amendment through Congress to that effect, but it failed. This was followed with a drive to call a constitutional convention, and thirty-three states joined the drives. This was only one short of the necessary thirty-four to call for a convention. They were never quite able to get the thirty-fourth state and the call then died on the vine.

We are in a similar situation today. We have a movement for a balanced budget amendment. Those who are supporting this movement are, for the most part, politically conservative. They are doing this believing Congress is irresponsible, out of control, and has moved away from the will of the people.

They can see Congress constantly passing legislation that requires massive and monstrous deficit spending. They feel the only way to get the economy under control, prevent an economic disaster, and place controls on congressional taxes is by following this check proposed by the Founding Fathers. The route of calling a constitutional convention bypasses Congress and puts in an amendment forcing Congress into following the will of the people and balancing the budget.

David — If Congress is unwilling to follow the will of the people today, then what is there in a constitutional convention that will change it? What is there about a constitutional convention that will force Congress to obey the dictates and the mandates of the people of the United States?

John — Your point is very well taken and I believe you've put your finger on one of the main flaws in the whole proposal. Frankly, I am very much opposed to a constitutional convention. I would favor a balanced budget amendment if it were brought through the traditional route of Congress. But, personally, I doubt it would be that effective. Already, there are several statutes on the books requiring Congress to balance the budget and they are routinely ignored. So I see little indication they would be any more impressed by a balanced budget amendment. Nevertheless, if it were passed, it might serve as a check on Congress. For that reason I would favor it. I don't really think it would restrain Congress in the manner it needs to be. The only way we can accomplish this is by electing a new Congress who are convinced of the need of fiscal responsibility. Until that happens, I don't think a constitutional convention, amendment, statute, or anything else will stop Congress.

David — Is it possible for delegates to such a convention to pass laws or enact legislation that would be counterproductive to us as Americans?

John — Let me answer that in the words of our former Chief Justice of the Supreme Court, Warren Burger, who was also chairman of the U.S. Bicentennial Commission. He notes that once the convention convenes, it will do whatever the majority of the convention wants to do. There isn't any way anyone could put a muzzle on it. And he said, "I would not favor it."

Let me quickly review how close we are or have been to calling a convention. As of a couple of years ago, thirty-two of the necessary thirty-four states had passed resolutions in their legislatures calling for a balanced budget amendment and calling for a constitutional convention. This was only two states short. During the last two or so years, two states, first Florida, then Alabama, have rescinded their calls for a convention. There might be some constitutional questions as to whether this will be held as valid, but it probably will be. This puts us now four states away from the necessary two-thirds. Therefore it is a present possibility and danger.

As to whether or not other amendments can be considered, we are being assured by those who are pushing for a constitutional convention that the convention will be subject to rules set by Congress and that the convention can consider only the subjects it is being convened to consider. This is the balanced budget amendment. But there is nothing in Article V that would give us any such assurances. Article V states that the convention can be called for the purpose of considering "amendments," in the plural form. According to one law professor, this is an indication the convention can consider anything they want.

There is supposedly one check in that, no matter what the convention may propose or pass, it can't become the law of the land until ratified by the various state legislatures. But we have a precedent that indicates otherwise, the Convention of 1787. If you read through the Continental Congress's call for that convention, we find they were to hold this convention for the purpose of considering amendments to the Articles of Confederation. When the convention began and a whole new constitution was proposed, several delegates questioned whether they had the authority to go beyond the call of the Continental Congress as they were doing. The majority held that so long as they proposed something, it was up to the states to ratify it. Therefore, they could propose anything and proceeded along that theory. They totally disregarded the mandates the Continental Congress had given them. When it came to the method of ratification, the Articles of Confederation in effect at the time provided that any amendment had to be approved by all thirteen states. If they had followed the mandated means of ratification they would never have succeeded, since Rhode Island didn't ratify it until several years later. The constitutional convention pulled another "end run" on the states and simply put in Article VII. Article VII provides that the Constitution would be effective when ratified by nine states. Therefore, if we had a new convention today, there is no guarantee it would be subject to any rules or restrictions placed by Congress. Neither is there any guarantee their recommendations would be approved by three-fourths of the states. They could set up their own means of ratification and implement the whole procedure through other means. This is a constitutional quagmire and is dangerous. When James Madison, whom many have called the Father of the Constitution, saw all the trials and tribulations that came out of the first convention and the ratification process following, he said, "I tremble at the prospect of a second convention." If he could see the direction society has gone in the last two hundred years, he'd tremble even more.

In my book *Christianity and the Constitution*, I demonstrate how the framers of our Constitution came from a Christian world view. They held a Christian view of man, believed man was a sinner, and held to the basic Calvinistic view of the depravity of human nature. For that reason, they feared giving too much power to sinful people. They had almost a paranoid, though totally justified, fear of government power. For that reason they were very careful to limit governmental powers and provide checks and balances for the various levels of government so that no one branch could become too powerful. This has been the genius of our constitutional system. It is based on a realistic view of the nature of man and his sinful propensities. This is the reason our Constitution has been extremely successful. I find no reason to believe those who would serve as delegates to a constitutional convention today would share that world view, that view of man, or the fear of governmental power.

I am very concerned what system of government they would propose. A number of groups have already proposed alternate constitutions. These would eliminate our system of checks and balances, making our system more like a European parliamentary system. This is extremely dangerous.

David — Let me point out the reason this is important to Christians. Our government is based on "We the people." As Christians and citizens of these United States under our present Constitution, it is our responsibility to operate the government according to biblical principals and the Christian world view you have been talking about. Most Christians fail to understand that we're not here to revolutionize the world or to take over, but as citizens, as "We the people," we have a responsibility to be informed and to act. We get criticized as Christians when we want to be informed and involved in our government. But we are the people and "We the people" must be involved in these issues.

John — I thoroughly agree. In fact, we read the government is ordained of God in Romans 13. One of the blessings God has given us in this nation is our ability to have some influence on policies of our government. God has established our government through the influence of godly men, and through a covenant these men made through the Constitution. Yes, this puts tremendous responsibility on all of us. In order to be effective, we need to recognize the current trend away from that world view and away from that system of government. This portends dangers of tyranny in the future.

There are many questions concerning the convention that are frightening to which no one has positive answers. One claim being made is that if thirty-four states call for the convention, there wouldn't have to be a convention. Congress would have the alternative of either passing the balanced budget amendment or calling for a convention. The language of Article V doesn't say that. It says that upon application of two-thirds of the states, Congress shall call a convention. Alexander Hamilton said there was no room for discussion here. The words are mandatory in nature and a Supreme Court decision not too long ago came to exactly the same conclusion. It's also being argued that Congress can set rules to govern the convention. First of all, we don't know of whom the convention will consist. Article V is silent about how the delegates are to be selected, who's to govern, what governing procedure they will follow, whether the Speaker of the House will be chairman, if members of Congress will be allowed to serve as delegates to this convention, whether they will be elected or appointed by the state governors, or just how they are to be chosen. After they propose their amendments, must they be approved by Congress first before going to the states? There are so many unanswered questions here that show the danger of this proceeding. I favor an amendment to Article V that would spell out these procedures. If these procedures were fully and clearly spelled out so we could have a constitutional convention clearly limited in what it could do and its power, and those limits were understood and recognized by everyone, then I could be inclined to favor a convention as a means of keeping Congress in check. As it is presently, it is a dangerous prospect.

There have been several proposals for statutes in Congress that would provide procedures in the event of a convention. None have yet become law since Congress can't agree on them. This being the case, what makes us think they could agree later?

David — What are some of the dangerous bits of legislation that might slip through the cracks of a convention like this?

John — One item proposed for consideration at this convention would be an Equal Rights Amendment. The ERA would supposedly end sex discrimination, mandate women in combat, and many other things. There is some indication there might be elections for the delegates. This could result in jockeying among the various power groups, including right-to-life and balanced-budget people, bartering with each other for stronger power in the convention itself. Coalitions like this would result in power struggles among the various groups as they try to get their people elected as delegates to the convention.

Among other proposals have been several new, totally redrafted constitutions. One I know of would change our system of government to what they are calling a "New States System." Under this proposal, instead of having fifty states, we would have "new states," regions, or administrative districts, to govern the nation.

Other proposals would eliminate many of the checks and balances in our present system, providing that Congress and the president would run on the same ticket, assuring whoever was in the White House would also control Congress since they work so closely together. This would pave the way for more powerful and restrictive legislation. Again, there are several proposals for a world constitution, eliminating the sovereignty of the United States, making us a part of a world government.

David — I've also heard something about declaring martial law to control the drug situation in the United States. Have you heard that?

John — I've only heard discussion concerning it and, of course, there are plenty of possibilities for that without a convention. This needs to be watched very carefully.

I feel that, although any or all of these techniques are proposed in innocence, they deprive us of our freedoms, establishing an authoritarian or totalitarian government. One way to accomplish this is to play upon a legitimate crisis, one that truly has people concerned. Certainly the drug epidemic in our nation today is a matter of concern for all of us. But playing on that concern are proposals to give extraordinary powers to the federal government. The problem is, once the need for that power goes away or is taken care of, the powers usually remain in effect. This technique is often used, either intentionally or unintentionally, as an excuse for extraordinary governmental powers which are the death knell of freedom.

David — Once that machinery is in place, there is no telling where it could go. Lately, we've been hearing a good deal about the Bill of Rights. In fact, there has been a touring display of an original copy of the Bill of Rights. Tell us what is happening concerning the Bill of Rights and this display.

John — We are moving into the final phases of the bicentennial celebration. This began back in 1976 with the celebration of the beginning of the Revolutionary War. Then in 1987 we had the two hundredth anniversary of the Constitutional Convention. We are approaching the closing days of the celebration. In 1989 the two hundredth anniversary of the ratification of the Constitution was observed. Now the Bill of Rights anniversary of adoption by Congress in 1789 and ratification in 1791, two hundred years ago this year.

David — The Bill of Rights guarantees some of our basic rights or freedoms, but some of these freedoms are at risk today. Tell us about some of these eroding freedoms we as Christians should be concerned about.

John — The display of the Bill of Rights touring the country during the Bicentennial Celebration of the ratification has been displayed in various cities around the country. This is one of the original copies along with quite an impressive and rather large display dealing with the history and background of the Bill of Rights. When it came through this area, I decided to take my family and to have my Constitutional Law students see it. Quite frankly, I was appalled and disgusted with what I saw. The propaganda gives a very distorted view of the Bill of Rights.

David — Propaganda?

John — That's right! This tour was sponsored by Phillip Morris, a tobacco company, along with Kraft Foods. The display consists of more than just the document. As you enter the display area there is a large picture of Thomas Jefferson. As far as I was able to see, that was the only portrait of any Founding Father on display. If you look at history, Jefferson wasn't even at the Constitutional Convention and had nothing to do with the Bill of Rights. During the entire period that the Constitution and the Bill of Rights were under consideration, he was serving as ambassador to France. Today's modern, liberal scholars like to resurrect their caricature of Thomas Jefferson since he fits their image of what a liberal is, more than any of the other Founding Fathers.

Continuing through the display, they do admit the Bill of Rights doesn't grant rights, only secures rights as we already have. I do appreciate that. They do not tell us the source of those rights. Even Jefferson had no hesitation telling us, as he put it in the Declaration of Independence, that "all men are <u>created</u> equal and are endowed by their Creator with certain unalienable rights." That is missing from this display.

Entering a hallway in the display area, they memorialize men and women who have had a major influence on our country with or through the Bill of Rights. Again, I was appalled at their choices. Every one of them were dedicated liberals, socialists, or communists.

For example, one display features Robert Baldwin. Mr. Baldwin is the founder and first president of the American Civil Liberties Union. He claimed openly his goal was communism. It also spoke of the ACLU, using glowing terms, as an organization willing to defend the liberties of all, regardless of the political ideology of the defendants.

Further down is a display featuring Margaret Sanger, an avowed racist. She is the founder of Planned Parenthood and saw as the purpose of Planned Parenthood the genocide of what she thought of and termed "inferior" races.

Also featured is Clarence Darrow. He was hired by the ACLU to defend evolution in the Scopes Trial. An interesting note here, he lost, but the display doesn't mention that.

I.F. Stone of the *I.F. Stone Weekly* is featured. We could continue down the line of these liberals, leftists, socialists, and communists, and not a single person is displayed whose views might reflect a conservative persuasion.

David — In other words, this display would tout pluralism here in the United States. We each should have the freedom to speak and to think as our conscience would dictate. Instead, they are touting a single philosophy which is out of touch with the will of the people. Am I correct?

John — Correct! They are using this display as a means of propagandizing the American public. You can misread the Bill of Rights as a very left-wing document if you wish to. The display portends the ACLU and the American left as having a monopoly on the Bill of Rights. They certainly do not.

David — There recently was a case here in Oklahoma where a child was told she no longer had the right to evangelize on the school grounds. She wasn't even to read the Bible or conduct Bible studies during recess time. There has been quite a controversy concerning it. Would this be covered in the Bill of Rights? And is it an erosion of our freedoms?

John — I think it is. We often speak of the Constitution as a living or an evolving document. By this is meant there are no absolute standards of right and wrong. He spoke of the laws of nature and the nature of God in the Declaration of Independence.

With this "evolving document" interpretation, we see the Supreme Court being freed to, as former Attorney General Edwin Meese put it, "roam at large in the trackless fields of their own imaginations." If the Supreme Court is not bound by the literal wording of the Constitution and by the intent of those who wrote it, then they are free to interpret it however they so desire. I'm reminded here by an illustration in Louis Carroll's book, *Through the Looking Glass*. In a conversation between Alice and Humpty Dumpty, Humpty Dumpty says, "When I use a word it means whatever I want it to mean, nothing more and nothing less." Alice asks, "Can you make words to mean whatever you want them to mean?" Humpty Dumpty answers, "The question is, 'Who is to be master?'

and that is all." He makes a wonderful point here. If judges are free to make the words of the Constitution and the Bill of Rights to mean whatever they want them to mean, the judges have become our masters.

Some areas where we see judges exerting that type of mastery over us are in the creation of new "rights" in the Constitution the founders never intended. For example, they speak of the right of abortion. Nowhere in the Constitution do you find that right mentioned or even alluded to. They also state it's part of our right to privacy. You don't see that term used in the Constitution either. When put to the point, they say, "Well, it's not specifically mentioned in there, but it's part of the penumbra of the Bill of Rights." By penumbra they mean a shadow, tail, or perhaps an aura. It's as if the liberal justices of the court are issued special colored glasses with which to look at the Constitution. They seem to see things written in the margins and between the lines the rest of us don't see. Some examples of these are: the right to engage in homosexual conduct and the right to an abortion.

Just as dangerous as this ability to read into the Constitution rights that aren't there, is their ability to read out of the Constitution rights that are there. They have already cut out any right to life for the unborn child. The Fourteenth Amendment guarantee of life applies only to people already born and is construed as having no application to the unborn. There is no support whatsoever for that conclusion. Other rights they regard as becoming less important include the right to enter into a contract, the right to own property and use it as one sees fit, the right to free exercise of religion, and the right to bear arms as guaranteed in the Second Amendment.

Other Books by Hearthstone Publishing

Now Is the Dawning of the New Age New World Order
by Dennis L. Cuddy
ISBN 1-879366-22-3   400 page book $14.95

Toward a New World Order Order
by Don McAlvany
ISBN 1-879366-26-6   250 page book $12.95

The Revived Roman Empire and the Beast of the Apocalypse
by N.W. Hutchings
ISBN 1-879366-31-2   140 pages $7.95

The Bill of Rights Cancelled
by Bill Uselton
ISBN 1-879366-33-9   30 page booklet $2.50

The Coming Persecution of the Church
by Don McAlvany
ISBN 1-879366-36-3   64 page booklet $5.00

What's Next?
by Keith J. Walsworth and Kenneth C. Hill
ISBN 1-879366-39-8   100 pages $6.95

An American Commentary
by Dennis L. Cuddy
ISBN 1-879366-40-1   250 pages $5.95

Confronting Our Nation's Problems
by Don McAlvany
ISBN 1-879366-47-9   30 page booklet $2.50

The Constitution Conspiracy
by Kenneth C. Hill and Bill Uselton
ISBN 1-879366-69-X   70 page booklet $2.50

To order, please call
1-800-652-1144